U.S. POLICY TOWARD THE BALTIC STATES

HEARING

BEFORE THE

SUBCOMMITTEE ON EUROPE, EURASIA, AND EMERGING THREATS

OF THE

COMMITTEE ON FOREIGN AFFAIRS HOUSE OF REPRESENTATIVES

ONE HUNDRED FIFTEENTH CONGRESS

FIRST SESSION

MARCH 22, 2017

Serial No. 115–11

Printed for the use of the Committee on Foreign Affairs

Available via the World Wide Web: http://www.foreignaffairs.house.gov/ or
http://www.gpo.gov/fdsys/

U.S. GOVERNMENT PUBLISHING OFFICE

24–752PDF   WASHINGTON : 2017

For sale by the Superintendent of Documents, U.S. Government Publishing Office
Internet: bookstore.gpo.gov   Phone: toll free (866) 512–1800; DC area (202) 512–1800
Fax: (202) 512–2104   Mail: Stop IDCC, Washington, DC 20402–0001

COMMITTEE ON FOREIGN AFFAIRS

EDWARD R. ROYCE, California, *Chairman*

CHRISTOPHER H. SMITH, New Jersey
ILEANA ROS-LEHTINEN, Florida
DANA ROHRABACHER, California
STEVE CHABOT, Ohio
JOE WILSON, South Carolina
MICHAEL T. McCAUL, Texas
TED POE, Texas
DARRELL E. ISSA, California
TOM MARINO, Pennsylvania
JEFF DUNCAN, South Carolina
MO BROOKS, Alabama
PAUL COOK, California
SCOTT PERRY, Pennsylvania
RON DeSANTIS, Florida
MARK MEADOWS, North Carolina
TED S. YOHO, Florida
ADAM KINZINGER, Illinois
LEE M. ZELDIN, New York
DANIEL M. DONOVAN, Jr., New York
F. JAMES SENSENBRENNER, Jr.,
 Wisconsin
ANN WAGNER, Missouri
BRIAN J. MAST, Florida
FRANCIS ROONEY, Florida
BRIAN K. FITZPATRICK, Pennsylvania
THOMAS A. GARRETT, Jr., Virginia

ELIOT L. ENGEL, New York
BRAD SHERMAN, California
GREGORY W. MEEKS, New York
ALBIO SIRES, New Jersey
GERALD E. CONNOLLY, Virginia
THEODORE E. DEUTCH, Florida
KAREN BASS, California
WILLIAM R. KEATING, Massachusetts
DAVID N. CICILLINE, Rhode Island
AMI BERA, California
LOIS FRANKEL, Florida
TULSI GABBARD, Hawaii
JOAQUIN CASTRO, Texas
ROBIN L. KELLY, Illinois
BRENDAN F. BOYLE, Pennsylvania
DINA TITUS, Nevada
NORMA J. TORRES, California
BRADLEY SCOTT SCHNEIDER, Illinois
THOMAS R. SUOZZI, New York
ADRIANO ESPAILLAT, New York
TED LIEU, California

AMY PORTER, *Chief of Staff*   THOMAS SHEEHY, *Staff Director*

JASON STEINBAUM, *Democratic Staff Director*

SUBCOMMITTEE ON EUROPE, EURASIA, AND EMERGING THREATS

DANA ROHRABACHER, California, *Chairman*

JOE WILSON, South Carolina
TED POE, Texas
TOM MARINO, Pennsylvania
JEFF DUNCAN, South Carolina
F. JAMES SENSENBRENNER, Jr.,
 Wisconsin
FRANCIS ROONEY, Florida
BRIAN K. FITZPATRICK, Pennsylvania

GREGORY W. MEEKS, New York
BRAD SHERMAN, California
ALBIO SIRES, New Jersey
WILLIAM R. KEATING, Massachusetts
DAVID N. CICILLINE, Rhode Island
ROBIN L. KELLY, Illinois

(II)

CONTENTS

U.S. POLICY TOWARD THE BALTIC STATES

WEDNESDAY, MARCH 22, 2017

HOUSE OF REPRESENTATIVES,
SUBCOMMITTEE ON EUROPE, EURASIA, AND EMERGING THREATS,
COMMITTEE ON FOREIGN AFFAIRS,
Washington, DC.

The subcommittee met, pursuant to notice, at 2:08 p.m., in room 2172, Rayburn House Office Building, Hon. Dana Rohrabacher (chairman of the subcommittee) presiding.

Mr. ROHRABACHER. Good afternoon. I call the subcommittee to order.

Today's hearing is focused on the Baltic region, U.S. policy to the countries of Estonia, Latvia, and Lithuania.

My colleagues in Congress, other opinion makers, and policy deciders often refer to the danger or conflict of this region. The reality of what has been happening or not happening in this corner of the world deserves a closer and, yes, a more comprehensive examination. And that is what this hearing is all about.

Our relationship with the Baltic people and governments has probably lasted 100 years. We have stood by those populations through the Soviet period in our firm support for the rights of Baltic people to freely choose their own governance and not have it dictated to them by the Nazis, the Communists, or anybody else.

Those who know me know how strongly I believe in self-determination. I am proud that American support helped these three Baltic countries reestablish their independence as communism collapsed in the Soviet Union. We stood by Estonia, Latvia, and Lithuania in the past, and they can be confident that we will remain the case in the future.

The citizens of the Baltics, like citizens in the Eastern Europe, are not pieces on a board for foreign policy powers to manipulate and to control. They are fully and equally sovereign nations.

Within that context, the Baltic nations were permitted to join NATO, which, as a consequence, has put troops that are a part of a hostile military alliance positioned right on Russia's border, a potential threat from Russia's perspective. Whatever you think about Russia today, it behooves us to act responsibly and to recognize that Russia too is a powerful nation, whose leaders make decisions based on their country's security and national interests. We do that, as well as every other major power.

However, the question today remains: Has Russia stepped over the bounds of acceptable behavior or has the U.S. been overreacting?

Since 2014, there have been numerous NATO exercises in the Baltics. And when we say that, that means we have had numerous NATO military exercises within a relatively short distance from St. Petersburg and Moscow and directly on the Russian border. Some of our witnesses today will help explain what is happening and what's been happening there in the Baltics and why. Knowing the facts of what is happening certainly will help us determine what America's policy toward this region should be, and what should our policy be toward Russia as well. But establishing the prerequisites for a peaceful world must remain a priority for us and for the Russians and for the people in the Baltics.

One thought. We here should do our best not to confuse a strong U.S. policy with a confrontational policy. What is the goal of peace through strength? It is not just strength. It is peace, and that we should never lose that perspective.

I welcome our witnesses this afternoon.

Without objection, your full written statements will be made part of the record.

So if you could, we would like to ask you to make a 5-minute presentation, and then we will move on to questions and dialogue with the panel and with the members.

I would like to focus on a few key questions. I would like to know about the specific acts that Russia is accused of doing in the Baltics. I don't want intentions. What are the specific acts that we should be most concerned about? And is our response to these specific acts reasonable or is it belligerent?

With that said, would ask my ranking member, Mr. Meeks, to move forward with his opening statement.

Mr. MEEKS. Thank you, Mr. Chairman, and thank you for calling today's hearing on U.S. policy regarding the Baltics. It is a region we do not always get to examine in detail, but do not often see in the news either.

Before my remarks, I would like to take a moment, though, to remember the attacks in Brussels just 1 year ago. And, today, we see a similar democracy being attacked again in London. It is a reminder that democracy is continuous, it is daily, and it is difficult. And we mourn those that may have lost their lives in the attack in London today.

The Baltics hold a special place in modern history. I admire their citizens for their peaceful, brave resistance to the Soviet regime during the nonviolent Singing Revolution. Soviet repression was not able to crush their cultures, their people, or their thirst for freedom. A beautiful story that one—and one that resonates here in the United States Congress.

The U.S. never recognized the Soviet occupation by force, and upon deliberation, they continued normal diplomatic relations. The same international laws compel us to never—today, to never recognize the Kremlin's attempt to annex Crimea.

In 1991, newly independent Lithuania, Latvia, Estonia, and— had to mature quickly in a dangerous post-Communist space where corruption, economic malice, and ethnic divisions were always a threat. The scars from the transformation can be seen and manipulated by outside actors today. Nevertheless, they are free. They reformed. They are banging on the doors to Europe saying, don't forget us. They are persistent. They joined NATO and the EU in 2004, and continue to play integral roles in both.

Estonia takes over the presidency of the council in July, and I look forward to learning more about their stories on the ground soon.

I am also a senior member of the Financial Services Committee and remember seeing the Baltic States suffer immensely during the financial crisis in 2008. Latvia saw its GDP shrink over 25 per-cent in less than a year, for example. The final result, a success story. Internal devaluation, belt tightening within an agreement between society and the government helped the small open econo-mies turn the corner and enjoy sustained growth. It was not easy, but the results are a best practice example for dealing with the euro crisis.

The Baltic States are also leaders in the internet age. I admire the Estonia movement, the dedicated push to bring the country to the forefront in e-commerce and e-democracy, where citizens can vote and register businesses online. I believe we have a few e-resi-dents in the crowd today.

However, this makes Estonia vulnerable to cyber attacks, which they have experienced, most notably in 2008. The result: Estonia is now home to the NATO Cyber Centre of Excellence, where all NATO member states can share and sharpen their skills in today's wide world.

The region is also a leader in the push toward energy trans-formation and independence. Seeing and feeling the way the Rus-sian Government uses energy as a political tool is a direct threat to the economies and populations in the Baltic States. A striking example is Lithuanian LNG terminal independence, which is only a part of a puzzle linking the region with a competitive supply of energy. Projects like this help Lithuania and Europe, both, from an energy and supply side and, importantly, from a security angle.

Finally, the success of the three states is an important symbol for those who need a united and free Europe. With NATO support, it is an important symbol for the region as an example of what can be achieved with membership in the transatlantic organizations that the guarantee of justice and the rule of law. Yet as the Baltic States continue to integrate and flourish as democracies, they are under threat. I do not believe that Russian tanks will roll across their borders, but the threat from the Kremlin is often subtle, often denied, in fact—or a post-fact world, but just as real and just as powerful. Their tools corrupt our information sphere, our econo-mies, and use cynicism only to protect kleptocracies in Moscow.

I believe we have an excellent panel here to examine these threats and discuss the best responses. I believe we must support the free press, much like we recently examined with Chairman Royce of the full committee level. And I also would like to examine the role, both symbolic and economic, of personal sanctions, specifi-cally, the Magnitsky Act, which goes after corrupt individuals, not the Russian people.

I am also an adamant supporter of NATO and the EU's role in values-based transatlantic relationship and how economies and people are better off with it.

To conclude, I would like to submit two excellent reads for the record that shaped what I am talking about today. President Reagan's Proclamation 4948, which created Baltic Freedom Day, and President Obama's speech in Tallinn in 2014. These documents show the continued bipartisan support for the Baltic States and the freedom and democracies that they bravely fought to establish.

I yield back.

Mr. ROHRABACHER. Well, thank you. And I sure appreciate you putting some of my writing into the work.

And then we have Mr. Fitzpatrick from Pennsylvania——

Mr. FITZPATRICK. Thank you, Mr. Chairman.

Mr. ROHRABACHER [continuing]. For 2 minutes.

Mr. FITZPATRICK. Yes, sir.

The fall of the USSR in 1991 ushered in a new era of freedom for many former Soviet Republics who had struggled for decades to maintain and express their national identities. The Baltic States of Latvia, Lithuania, and Estonia are prime examples of the demise of the Soviet Union and how the demise of the Soviet Union led to a freer and more independent Europe.

After gaining their independence in the summer of 1991, the Baltic States began to craft their own economies, their own militaries, and even more importantly, their own identities. This is something that we as Americans should all appreciate.

The Baltic States also desire to become part of the integrated global community by becoming both members of NATO as well as the European Union. However, in recent years, the Russian bear has once again reared its ugly head. We first saw this in 2008 when the Russian army invaded its fiercely independent southern neighbor, Georgia. In a quick but brutal war, the Russians showed what lengths they were willing to go in order to exert their dominance over their newly independent neighbors.

Likewise, in 2014, Vladimir Putin covertly moved Russian military forces into the Crimean region, quickly seizing it. Subsequent that year, the Russian-backed insurgency began to take hold of the eastern Donbass region in the Ukraine, culminating in the shoot-down of a Malaysian Airlines flight under very suspicious circumstances, this all being done with limited intervention from previous administrations;

As we look forward, it is imperative that we maintain our relationship with critical allies in the Baltic States. We must reassert America's commitment to prevent the rise of another Soviet block where a country's leaders are beholding to Moscow and not their own people.

I yield back.

Mr. ROHRABACHER. And now Brad.

All right, Brad, you are first.

Mr. SHERMAN. Okay. I want to associate myself with the comments of the ranking member recognizing the people of Belgium and the people of the United Kingdom and what they have suffered, and his praise for the Baltic States.

The foreign policy establishment has spoken. Everything that Putin does is wrong and, therefore, anything done by anyone in conflict with Putin must be right. I will spend a few minutes questioning that second assumption. The Baltic States are, indeed, praiseworthy, but they can and should do better.

I have been in this room for 20 years, and for most of that time, the foreign policy establishment said anyone who focused on burden sharing was ignorant or worse. Now, they have caved in on that and, instead, clung to this 2 percent standard. It should be a 4 percent standard. America spends over 4 percent of our GDP on our military. The foreign policy establishment deliberately understates that by ignoring the cost of the veterans benefits which, after all, are compensation we provide our soldiers and sailors.

Unfortunately, only one of the Baltic States even meets the 2 percent requirement, and the others—one other is saying they will get to it eventually, but that leaves their armaments way too low a level because, for decades, they have been underspending. Baltic States should at least match our 4 percent level and make up for the armaments they don't have because they've deliberately underspent for decades.

NATO is important. Only one NATO country has been attacked during NATO, and that is the United States. We had support in Afghanistan. The support from the Baltic States was there, but incredibly modest. In contrast, the Baltic States have asked us for an incredibly robust response to the national security threats that they face, including, as the chairman points out, deploying American soldiers by the thousands on the Russian border.

In the United Nations, I have been disappointed with the Baltic States support for us, voting against us again and again and again in the general assembly, though I support the recent support of two of the Baltic States in one UNESCO vote.

And, finally, we need to urge the Baltic States to treat the Russian minorities with as much respect as possible and more respect than maybe popular in their own political—among their own people, especially the Estonian issue with so many citizens of Estonia or residents of Estonia not be—having Estonian passports, not being recognized as citizens. I would hope that there would be a system that would allow dual citizenship and allow these folks to have whatever rights Russia chooses to grant them, but to have all the rights of Estonian citizens.

There are many arguments on both sides as to how the Russian-speaking minority should be treated, but since this could be a flashpoint for a major war, I would hope the Baltic States would err on the side of treating their Russian-speaking minority well.

And I yield back.

Mr. ROHRABACHER. Thank you, Mr. Sherman.

And now, Mr. Cicilline.

Mr. CICILLINE. Thank you, Chairman Rohrabacher and Ranking Member Meeks for calling this hearing today and to the witnesses for being here to discuss a region that is vital to America's strategic national security interests.

Lithuania, Latvia, and Estonia are located at Russia's doorstep and, in many ways, are at the forefront in the increasing tensions in Eastern Europe. Each of these states serves as an example of the ability of the people to rise out of the chaos of the fall of the Soviet Union, embrace democracy and free markets, and thrive.

Formerly members of the Warsaw Pact, as part of the Soviet Union today, Estonia, Latvia, and Lithuania are vital members of NATO. And perhaps no countries face a graver challenge from the renewed aggression of Putin's Russia. The invasions of Georgia and Ukraine have caused many within the Baltics to fear for their own sovereignty as Putin attempts to delegitimize states that have a large Russian-speaking population. And that is why it is so important that the United States not waiver in our commitment to the NATO alliance and to our Baltic friends to ensure that the ties we have forged remain strong in the face of increased pressure.

I look forward to hearing from our witnesses today. And I want to apologize in advance, we have a Judiciary Committee markup, so I will be in and out. But I'm anxious to hear what we can do to reinforce and strengthen our NATO commitments and to continue the strong relationships the United States has built with our Baltic friends. I thank you.

And I yield back, Mr. Chairman.

Mr. ROHRABACHER. Well, thank you very much.

And I would like to thank the witnesses for joining us today. I will introduce all of you, and then we will proceed.

First, we have Paul Goble, who is a long-time expert in minority nationalities and the former Soviet Union. He has had a distinguished career working at various times for the United States Government, the State Department, as well as Radio Free Europe. He has been honored by the governments of all three Baltic republics for his efforts to promote their independence.

Lisa Sawyer Samp or Sap?

Ms. SAMP. Samp.

Mr. ROHRABACHER. Samp. Okay. A senior fellow in the Internation Security Program at the Center for Strategic and International Studies. She is an expert on NATO and European defense strategies. And before joining CSIS, she was in a previous role as director for NATO and European Strategic Affairs on the National Security Council staff.

We have Matthew Rojansky. He is the director of the Kennan Institute at the Woodrow Wilson Center. He is a leading expert on U.S.-Russian relations and an adjunct professor at Johns Hopkins.

He serves as U.S. executive secretary for the Dartmouth Conference which is a two-track of the Russian-U.S. conflict resolution initiative. I hope I got that exactly right, but you get the picture. Mr. Edward Lucas is a senior editor for The Economist. And I might add,

I read that magazine all the time. I think it is, frankly, the only magazine I do read all the time. He is a senior vice president at the Center for European Policy Analysis. He has been observing and writing about developments in Eastern Europe and that part of the world for over 20 years.

So we are very pleased to have you and grateful to have you with us. So, as I say, if you could proceed with 5-minute opening statements or you could add to that, just for the record, and then we will proceed with questions from the members.

Mr. Goble.

STATEMENT OF MR. PAUL A. GOBLE, PRINCIPAL PROFESSOR, THE INSTITUTE OF WORLD POLITICS

Mr. GOBLE. Thank you, Mr. Chairman. Thank you for calling this hearing on this most important topic and for giving me an opportunity to appear.

I would like to dedicate my remarks to the late Aleksander Einseln, the Estonian-American colonel, who died about 10 days ago, who went to Estonia and became the commander of the Estonian Defence Forces and played a key role in transforming those forces into ones that could be integrated into the Western alliance. It is an ancient observation that old generals always prepare to fight the last war, but we don't always think about what that means. It often means that they look for the same kind of threat that happened in the past and try to counter it, or not seeing it, decide there isn't any threat at all, and that they fail to prepare for combating new threats, because the means they have adopted in the past to counter the threats of the past are no longer the ones that are most important.

I do not believe, as long as Estonia, Latvia, and Lithuania are a members of the western alliance, that any Russian Government will send its tanks over the eastern borders of those countries. I think that is almost unthinkable because I think it is almost certainly suicidal.

Having said that, however, I believe there is a very real Russian threat that flows both from the purposes that Mr. Putin has announced for his government going back more than a decade and the means he has chosen to use to pursue those purposes.

On the one hand, Mr. Putin has clearly signaled that the three—that his foreign policy is driven by a desire to challenge the three bedrock principles of the international system that the United States took the lead in forming in the 20th century. First, the 1919 settlement that declared that the Arab empires is over. He wants to restore one. Second, the settlement of 1945, which held that citizenship is more important than ethnicity. That is what we fought World War II about when the Germans thought that ethnicity was more important than citizenship. And 1991, when the international community accepted the demise of the USSR as something that was irreversible.

But the other aspect of the Russian threat is also serious, and that is that Mr. Putin has chosen to use the strategies of subversion rather than the strategies of open force. Far more often we have seen actions by the Russian Government that are those of intelligence services rather than those of defense ministries. What that means is if you are looking for actions by the military, you won't find them, but if you are looking at what goes on in banks, in government offices, in propaganda outlets, they are very much there.

Estonia, Latvia, and Lithuania have particular reasons for being concerned about both Mr. Putin's goals—if any of those are realized, they would be at risk—and his tactical approach because of their size and their propinquity to Russia. We in the United States tend to forget how small the Baltic countries are, how much they suffered under various aspects of Russian rule, and how much they have depended on the United States.

For Putin, those three realities have a contradictory message. On the one hand, they mean that Mr. Putin is certainly aware that any military move against the Baltic countries would be resisted by the United States as part of its NATO alliance and, second, it means that Mr. Putin has an interest in challenging the West precisely there as a way of indicating that the West is more of a paper tiger than the West believes.

I believe that what we need to do in order to promote Baltic security has less to do with the expansion of NATO presence there, although I welcome that presence, than it does with doing other things. And I would like to suggest three of what would be a very large list.

First, as several of the members have pointed out, we need to encourage all three countries to complete the integration of ethnic minorities in their countries, that the progress that has been made is truly amazing. Indeed, last week, it was announced that there are 4,000 ethnic Russians in Estonia who now declare that Estonian is their native language, which is—would have been unthinkable a decade ago. That is an impressive achievement. Second, we need to promote transparency of all economic and political activities, banking, the communication sector. And, third, we need to involve Estonians, Latvians, Lithuanians in as many conversations as possible with Russian counterparts.

There are people in the West who are not interested in pushing that, who prefer to see the question of Russian power as being one that there is only a military response to. But, in fact, it is in these other areas that the fight is going to be won or lost, and, therefore, we should be spending far more time developing strategies in those areas than in others.

Thank you very much.

[The prepared statement of Mr. Goble follows:]

New Threats Require a New Response:
What the Baltic Countries and the US Face in Putin's Russia

Paul A. Goble
Institute of World Politics

Testimony Prepared for a Hearing on US Policy toward the Baltic States,
US House of Representatives Committee on Foreign Affairs'
Sub-Committee on Europe, Eurasia and Emerging Threats
March 22, 2017
Washington, D.C.

It is an ancient observation that old generals always prepare to fight the last war over again, an attitude that ensures that they either dismiss real threats because they aren't the ones they expected or fail to prepare to combat new threats in an effective way and thus suffer far larger losses than would have been the case had they focused on current realities than past memories.

That is currently a serious risk that the United States and its Baltic allies run in coping with the threat posed by Vladimir Putin. Because there is little chance that Moscow will send its tanks and planes into Estonia, Latvia and Lithuania, all of whom are members of NATO, many are inclined to conclude that there is no Russian threat there at all and that those in the Baltic countries, Europe and the United States who say otherwise are being alarmist.

But in fact, Putin poses a far greater threat to the Baltic countries and to the West more generally not only because of the goals that he has clearly articulated over the last decade but also because of the means he has adopted to promote them, means that unfortunately neither NATO nor many NATO member countries are focusing on or developing the kind of policies that will effectively defend them against these threats.

Here, I would like to focus on three things: the nature of the Russian threat to the West, the reasons the Baltic countries have for particular concern about this threat, and the common interest the United States has in countering that threat, including three suggestions concerning what the Baltic countries and the United States should be doing together to ensure that Putin will not succeed in his approach in the Baltic region -- and additionally to prevent him from taking actions elsewhere that would be likely to lead to a broader war.

The Dual Nature of the Russian Threat

There are two aspects to the current Russian threat to the West and both need to be kept in mind. On the one hand, there are the three bedrock principles of the international system that Vladimir Putin wants to tear up: the 1919 settlement that declared that the era of empires is over, the 1945 one that held that citizenship is more important than ethnicity in the organizing of political space, and the 1991 outcome which held that the demise of the USSR was something that could be reversed only with the most adverse consequences for the peoples of that region and the broader world.

And on the other, Putin's approach at both the strategic and tactical level is that of an intelligence operative rather than a statesman. He has pursued a policy of subversion against his neighbors and other countries further afield, including propaganda, bribery and corruption, and support for those who favor chaos over those who favor any order opposed to him. The Kremlin leader and others call this a "hybrid" war, one that doesn't look like a real one and that gives him plausible deniability in many cases. What is critical here is not that other governments have not on occasion used these same tactics but rather that Putin has made them central to his foreign policy and that none of the existing security arrangements in the world is adequate to opposing them.

Thus, NATO could stop Russian tanks that may never come; but it is not organized to deal with this strategy of subversion which is already too much in evidence in various countries, including our own. In many ways, what Putin has done recalls what others in a position of weakness always try to do: they select means that their opponents have not focused on trying to counter. Just as terrorism is the weapon of the weak primarily among non-state actors around the world, subversion is the weapon of the weak among states.

Why the Baltic Countries have Particular Reason for Concern

Estonia, Latvia and Lithuania have particular reasons for being concerned about both Putin's political goals and his tactical approach. On the one hand, they are three small countries bordering an enormously large Russian Federation, whose existence and flourishing represents an obstacle to Putin's achievement of at least two and possibly three of his goals. And on the other, their size and ethnic diversity, especially in Estonia and Latvia, open the way for Russian subversion via corruption, propaganda, and economic pressure. Indeed, as Moscow has recognized since 1991, making use of these tactics with regard to the Baltic countries is far more effective than any direct military threat that NATO and the West might counter.

It is difficult for Americans to remember three things about the Baltic countries: how really small they are, how much they have suffered under various periods of Russian rule, and how much they have depended on the United States, first and foremost for Washington's non-recognition policy while they were under Soviet occupation but also for the support the US has given to them, far more than to any former Soviet republic, in the last 25 years since they recovered their independence.

For Putin, the connections of the Baltic countries with the West in general and the US in particular have a dual set of consequences. Clearly, these ties mean that the Kremlin leader is very much aware that any direct military attack on any or all of the three would lead to disaster for Russia in the first instance, even if some in Washington now are incautious enough to suggest otherwise. But these links between Estonia, Latvia and Lithuania and the US and the West also make them a tempting target for subversion. If Putin can undermine these countries and their remarkable progress both domestically and internationally, he will not only show all the former Soviet republics that they have little chance of success but that the West is a paper tiger even with regard to those it has committed itself to defend.

Hence, Putin has chosen the path of subversion. His government has corrupted the political and banking systems in these countries to an unprecedented degree. His propagandists have played up ethnic issues in all three countries but especially in Estonia and Latvia despite the success Tallinn and Riga have had in integrating the ethnic Russians there. And the constant refrain of Moscow propagandists that Estonia, Latvia and Lithuania are not "real states" but rather colonies of the West can only be troubling to them – even if there are NATO boots on the ground and NATO planes in the air over them.

How the US Can Promote New Ways to Help the Baltic Countries

I was an early advocate of including Estonia, Latvia and Lithuania in NATO and the European Union, and I believe that these memberships have been incredibly important for allowing these countries to develop as free and democratic ones and for preventing the rise of populist nationalist and anti-Russian forces that would feed on the fears of Russia that would be far larger if the three were not part of the West.

But having said that, I believe that there are many things we should be doing to promote Baltic security that have nothing to do with NATO or our own military. Let me suggest just three: First of all, we should encourage the three countries to complete the integration of the ethnic minorities in their countries as rapidly as possible so that Moscow will not be able to use that as a wedge issue to divide them.

Second, we should promote transparency of all economic and political activities in the three and especially work to promote Internet security on which the economies and polities of the three increasingly depend. Estonia, Latvia and Lithuania have taken giant steps in this direction but they need our help. Ensuring transparency of economic and political activity and guaranteeing computer security in Tallinn, Riga and Vilnius are almost certainly more important than putting more troops on the ground.

And third, we should promote in every possible way conversations between the Estonian, Latvian and Lithuanian government and society with their opposite numbers in Russia. That is doubly important: These countries can't afford to be in a hostile relationship with Moscow forever – and eventually even Putin will pass from the scene – especially given the current unwillingness of the West to stand against the Kremlin leader's aggressiveness. And by seeking such conversations, together with their Scandinavian and East European partners, they can at least highlight where the problems in relations lie and perhaps over time even promote positive changes in the dictatorship that is Russia today.

***

At present, the US is divided between those who think that Putin is not a threat to us and those who believe he is an existential one. Those who believe that he represents an immediate threat to the United States are almost certainly wrong given the weaknesses of his country, but those who argue that he is not a threat at all forget that aggressive regimes like his, even if they are weak, may conclude that they can press their case if there is no willingness to combat them at the early stages of their resurgence.

The West did not respond forcefully to the Russian invasion of Georgia in 2008, despite that war being the direct result of the policies that Vladimir Putin articulated at the Munich Security Conference a year earlier. And it has not found a way to counter Putin's aggression in Ukraine, which began in 2014 with the Anschluss of Crimea and which continues to this day not only in the Russian-occupied Donbass but throughout Ukraine as a whole.

Putin clearly thinks he is on a winning streak, and dictators who draw that conclusion often plunge the world into a broader war if they are not countered in time. The experience of Britain in the 1930s is particularly instructive in this regard. In 1938, Prime Minister Nevil Chamberlain justified his policy of "positive appeasement" with Hitler by saying that "small countries far away about which we know little" should not expect the great powers to "come to their rescue anytime they get in trouble" with larger neighbors.

That policy and that attitude, of course, led Hitler to assume that he could ignore British and French commitments to Poland; and that error in judgment by the Nazi leader thus led to the outbreak of World War II in Europe.

It is not too much to say now that those who oppose supporting Estonia, Latvia and Lithuania against Russian threats are engaged in the same act of self-delusion as the pre-war British prime minister. We must recognize that the defense of the three Baltic countries like the defense of Czechoslovakia in 1938 is not just about three "small countries" far away and is not just about military alliances alone. Instead, we must recognize that countering the new threats that Putin's Russia poses is the proper defense of the entire international system against its destruction, an outcome that is just as much in the interests of the United States as it is of Estonia, Latvia and Lithuania.

Mr. ROHRABACHER. Ms. Samp, you may go right ahead.

STATEMENT OF MS. LISA SAWYER SAMP, SENIOR FELLOW, INTERNATIONAL SECURITY PROGRAM, CENTER FOR STRATEGIC AND INTERNATIONAL STUDIES

Ms. SAMP. Mr. Chairman, Ranking Member Meeks, and distinguished members of the subcommittee, good afternoon.

I would like to make just two points regarding the current security situation in the Baltic States. My first point is foundational to this discussion. Russia is a threat. Russia is a threat to the Baltic States and, more broadly, to the post-World War II international order.

In the Baltics, Russia has conducted cyber attacks, crossborder kidnappings, and unannounced snap exercises with up to 80,000 troops just across the border. It has also violated their sovereign airspace, issued hostile statements, and filled their airwaves with propaganda.

For an accurate threat picture, though, this behavior must be considered in the context of what Moscow has done and is doing beyond the Baltics. In addition to meddling in foreign elections, violating arms control agreements, and nuclear saber rattlings, Putin's bullying has escalated to the use of military force in Georgia, Ukraine, and Syria.

In Ukraine, he has annexed Crimea and continues to sow instability and violence in the country's east. Thousands have died and over a million have been displayed. Let us also please not forget about the 298 civilians who were killed when a Russian-provided missile brought down a civilian airliner, or about the thousands of civilians killed by indiscriminate Russian bombs in Syria.

Russia's actions reflect an effective blending of both conventional and unconventional tactics. These tactics are designed to circumvent U.S. and NATO redlines, confuse traditional response options, and use the virtues of the West against it.

Putin likely doesn't want a war with the West, but he is finding he can get a lot done without one. For that reason, he has no intention of stopping now. He is becoming more emboldened over time and growing increasingly comfortable taking risks. What was once primarily an eastern-flank challenge is now hitting closer to home. Moscow may no longer be motivated by a Communist ideology that sees it trying to overthrow democracies and replace them with dictatorships. But that does not mean Russia isn't still a threat to our democracy and our institutions.

The difference today is that instead of offering an alternative, Russia is satisfied to create chaos and sow instability. It wants to knock the United States down a peg and break Western unity so we can't call shots Russia doesn't like or hold it accountable to the rule of law.

The system, though, that Russia is seeking to undermine has served the United States well over the past 70 years. And without it, the world would undoubtedly be poorer, less free, and less safe. Russia may just be looking out for what it considers to be in its national interests, but then we need to do the same, and that entails pushing back to protect ourselves, our allies, and the international order.

This brings me to my second point, which is that the steps taken by the United States and NATO to bolster security in the region are prudent and are what is minimally required. They are neither hostile nor provocative.

While Russia has not resorted to military force in the Baltics, and while its ever doing remains extremely unlikely, the possibility cannot be discounted completely. To manage this risk, the United States and NATO have taken steps, as described in my written testimony, to establish a credible deterrence. Far from being provocative, these steps are designed to prevent war and to make clear the costs that would be entailed with any aggression. It may, in fact, be more provocative to do nothing. To invite Russian opportunism by baiting it would weak defenses.

While it is important to debate what constitutes credible deterrence and what amounts to unhelpful provocation, one can also err in being too cautious, lending credence to Russia's reflexive protests and false indignation. I would argue there exists a wide gulf between the steps that have been taken to date and the steps that could be taken in the future to increase the West's leverage without sparking a conflict or even coming close.

Step back and recall, for example, that despite recent troop increases, the U.S. combat presence in Europe remains a full brigade-strength below what it was in 2012, prior to renewed tensions with Russia, and that NATO's largest exercise conducted since the end of the Cold War included about 30,000 troops. By contrast, Russia's Zapad exercise planned for later this year may reach up to 200,000. Thus, the idea that holding relatively moderately sized exercises on alliance territory constitutes provocation seems wildly unfair.

NATO is also not the ones flying with its transponders off, failing to announce exercises in accordance with the Vienna document, and buzzing ships in the Black and Baltic Seas. While it is also fair to consider the West's role in contributing to the current standoff with Russia, suggesting moral equivalencies or assigning blame does not solve the current problem. It neither changes how the West or Russia view their security interests nor makes what we seek to preserve any less valid.

To conclude, none of this means we cannot still cooperate with Russia where it is in our interest, but rushing to make deals with Moscow to secure what would amount to short-term gains may well end up sacrificing more fundamental goals.

Thank you.

[The prepared statement of Ms. Samp follows:]

CSIS | CENTER FOR STRATEGIC & INTERNATIONAL STUDIES

Statement before the

House Foreign Affairs Committee

Subcommittee on Europe, Eurasia, and Emerging Threats

"U.S. Policy toward the Baltic States"

A Testimony by:

Lisa Sawyer Samp

Senior Fellow,

International Security Program,

Center for Strategic and International Studies (CSIS)

March 22, 2017

2172 Rayburn House Office Building

WWW.CSIS.ORG   1616 RHODE ISLAND AVENUE NW | TEL: (202) 887.0200
WASHINGTON, DC 20036 | FAX (202) 775.3199

Chairman Rohrabacher, Ranking Member Meeks, and distinguished Members of the Subcommittee, it is an honor to testify before you today with my colleagues Paul Goble, Edward Lucas, and Matthew Rojansky on U.S. policy toward the Baltic States.

This testimony is informed by two studies conducted in my capacity as a Senior Fellow at the Center for Strategic and International Studies: (1) "Evaluating Future U.S. Army Force Posture in Europe," released in June 2016; and (2) "Perspectives on Security and Strategic Stability: A Track 2 Dialogue with Poland and the Baltic States," released in October 2016. This testimony also draws from research and analysis informing a forthcoming report, "Recalibrating U.S. Strategy toward Russia: A New Time for Choosing," which will be published in late March 2017, as well as from my previous experience working European security issues on the National Security Council Staff and at the Department of Defense.

My testimony will focus on the security and defense aspects of U.S. policy toward the Baltic States. I have strived to introduce key terms and concepts without getting overly technical regarding NATO processes.

Summary

Following Russia's invasion of Ukraine in 2014, the Baltic States—Estonia, Latvia, and Lithuania—were quickly elevated as a U.S. defense priority. This was due not only to their multiple requests for assistance based on a perceived vulnerability vis-à-vis Russia, but also due to the emerging recognition within Washington that the NATO alliance, following a decade of expeditionary operations in Afghanistan and elsewhere, had likely underappreciated the need to take appropriate precautions for deterrence and defense in Europe's own backyard. While policymakers and analysts continued to assess the likelihood of Russia using military force against the Baltic States as extremely low, none could discount the possibility completely given "Moscow's aggressive foreign policy and pattern of military intervention along its borders, combined with the strategic vulnerability of NATO's eastern allies, particularly the Baltic States...[whose militaries] are small, geographically isolated, and lack mobility, firepower, and air and naval capability."[1] Thus, a consensus emerged that more needed to be done, and quickly, to manage the extremely high risks at play in the region. In many ways, the credibility of allies' Article 5 commitment became tied to their response in the Baltic States.

The United States became the first to respond by surging air, land, and sea forces into Eastern Europe. The immediate U.S. deployment sent a strong signal of resolve to Moscow, calmed nervous allies, and initiated what would become an alliance-wide reassurance effort that included additional force presence, enhanced training and exercises, prepositioned equipment, and infrastructure improvements. Since that time, the United States and its allies have begun to transition from reassurance-focused measures to those that seek to establish a longer-term credible deterrence. This includes, among other things, expanding the number of troops in each Baltic State from a company-sized force (approximately 150 troops) to a more capable battalion-sized force (approximately 1,000 multinational troops); updating war plans; reconfiguring

---

[1] Kathleen Hicks, Heather Conley, Lisa Sawyer Samp, and Anthony Bell, *Evaluating Future U.S. Army Force Posture in Europe: Phase II Report* (Washington, DC: Center for Strategic and International Studies, June 2016), 48, https://csis-prod.s3.amazonaws.com/s3fs-public/publication/160712_Samp_ArmyForcePostureEurope_Web.pdf.

prepositioned equipment to support war plan requirements (as opposed to training and exercises); standing up a rapid reaction force that would be able to quickly surge reinforcements in a crisis; establishing eight reception and staging centers along NATO's eastern flank to receive those reinforcements; updating alliance threat assessments; improving logistics to reduce barriers to the freedom of movement for troops and equipment across Europe; and reinvesting in the defense capabilities needed for territorial defense.

Much of the U.S. contribution to broader NATO assurance and deterrence efforts—known collectively as the Readiness Action Plan—has been funded by the European Reassurance Initiative (ERI) and conducted under the auspices of the Defense Department's Atlantic Resolve mission. ERI was initiated in fiscal year (FY) 2015 as a $1 billion appropriation within the Defense Department's Overseas Contingency Operations (OCO) budget.[2] Former President Obama's FY 2017 budget request proposed quadrupling ERI funding to $3.4 billion, up from $789 million in FY 2016, in acknowledgement of the growing threat Russia poses to U.S. interests in Europe. Despite continuing to reside in the one-year OCO budget, ERI is now considered a multi-year effort aimed at enhancing the U.S. presence, capability, and readiness in Europe after decades of decline. ERI does not aspire to return the United States to a Cold War-era posture. It does, however, aim to allow the United States to better defend its interests and allies and to begin to contend with Russia's military advantages in Eastern Europe by taking steps deemed minimally necessary for credible deterrence. These steps are prudent given the security environment and are neither hostile nor provocative toward Russia, despite Moscow's reflexive cries to the contrary.

All of these efforts—and how they fit together in a conventional reinforcement strategy—are explored in greater detail below.

About the Baltic States

The context of history, demographics, geography, and size matter greatly when trying to understand the threat perceptions and vulnerabilities of the Baltic States. While there are many factors that make each state unique, Estonia, Latvia, and Lithuania's shared experience under approximately 50 years of Soviet occupation—a traumatic period replete with "mass exiles, forced collectivization, linguistic-cultural Russification, and attempts to extinguish their national identities"—led to a common drive for liberation in the late 1980s.[3] Citizens from across the region famously formed a human "Baltic Chain" to demonstrate against Soviet rule in 1989. Despite violent crackdowns in Lithuania and Latvia, all three Baltic States obtained their independence in 1991, setting into motion a gradual lurch westward that culminated in 2004 with their accession to both the European Union and NATO.

---

[2] White House, "Fact Sheet: European Reassurance Initiative and Other U.S. Efforts in Support of NATO Allies and Partners," June 3, 2014, https://obamawhitehouse.archives.gov/the-press-office/2014/06/03/fact-sheet-european-reassurance-initiative-and-other-us-efforts-support-.

[3] Lisa Sawyer Samp, Jeffrey Rathke, and Anthony Bell, *Perspectives on Security and Strategic Stability: A Track 2 Dialogue with the Baltic States and Poland* (Washington, DC: Center for Strategic and International Studies, October 2016), 3, https://csis-prod.s3.amazonaws.com/s3fs-public/publication/161007_Samp_PerspectivesSecurity_Web.pdf.

One legacy of the Soviet occupation is the large ethnic Russian minority populations that reside in each state. Ethnic Russians account for approximately 25 percent of the population in Estonia, 26 percent in Latvia, and 6 percent in Lithuania.[4] The political influence of these minority groups varies by country, with Latvia's center-left Harmony party generally considered to be the strongest and most closely aligned with Putin's United Russia party.[5] Moscow uses the presence of these minority populations as both pretext for continued involvement in the Baltic States and as soft targets for propaganda and other influence efforts meant to destabilize and undermine the central government (and NATO more broadly). Debate remains, however, among scholars and experts in the Baltic States over the degree to which these populations are susceptible to Russia's meddling. Regardless, there is little question over the fact that Russia is currently engaged in unconventional or so-called hybrid activities in the Baltic States, including cyber attacks, military intimidation, media manipulation, political subversion, and energy coercion.

Geographically, the Baltic States are the most military exposed to Russia of any NATO ally. Estonia and Latvia border the Russian mainland to the east, and Lithuania is situated between Kaliningrad to the west and Belarus to the east with only the narrow 60-mile Suwalki Gap with Poland connecting the region to the rest of the alliance. This geographic reality, combined with the size and capability of the Russian military, create an unavoidable time and space disadvantage for NATO in attempting to defend the Baltic States. In a crisis, Russia could likely overwhelm and occupy them in a matter of days. This is not to suggest that the Baltic militaries are subpar fighting forces, but simply that they are small. Consider, for example, that the Latvian and Estonian militaries total only 5,000 and 6,000 troops respectively, which combined is less than half of the daily population of the Pentagon.[6]

Despite their small size, the Baltic militaries have been able to cultivate niche specialties that add valuable capabilities to the NATO alliance. For example, Estonia has emerged as a leading member of the alliance in terms of cyber defense, Latvia has developed a strong capability in joint terminal attack controllers and explosive ordnance disposal, and Lithuania has robust special operations forces.[7] Estonia is also one of only five NATO allies that meet the recommended two percent of GDP defense spending target ($497 million in 2016), with Latvia and Lithuania on track to meet the goal by 2018. All three countries have sent troops to Iraq and Afghanistan.

Even with these investments, however, the Baltic States' size, limited military capabilities, and geographic proximity to Russia will keep them almost entirely dependent on the United States and NATO for their national defense in a conventional conflict—a fact which they publicly acknowledge. For this reason, much of the United States' relationship with the Baltic States is heavily weighted toward bilateral security cooperation and activities within NATO. Until the Ukraine crisis, NATO's primary contribution to Baltic security—aside from its Article 5

---

[4] "Estonia," "Latvia," and "Lithuania," *The World Factbook* (Washington, DC: Central Intelligence Agency, 2016), https://www.cia.gov/library/publications/the-world-factbook/.

[5] "How to Deal with Harmony," *The Economist*, October 6, 2014. http://www.economist.com/blogs/easternapproaches/2014/10/latvias-election.

[6] NATO, Public Diplomacy Division, "Defence Expenditures of NATO Countries (2008–2015)," January 28, 2016, http://www.nato.int/nato_static_fl2014/assets/pdf/pdf_2016_01/20160129_160128-pr-2016-11-eng.pdf.

[7] Samp et al., *Perspectives on Security and Strategic Stability: A Track 2 Dialogue with the Baltic States and Poland*, 21.

guarantees, of course—was the **Baltic Air Policing (BAP)** mission, which began in 2004 to protect the integrity of alliance airspace. BAP is one of the missions that have been augmented since 2014 to include more fighter aircraft operating out of additional air bases in the Baltics.

Establishing Credible Deterrence in NATO's East

In addition to economic and diplomatic actions taken in response to the crisis in Ukraine, the United States quickly established an enhanced and persistent air, land, and sea presence in Eastern Europe and, in June 2014, proposed the establishment of the $1 billon **European Reassurance Initiative** to fund activities across five categories: (1) presence; (2) training and exercises; (3) infrastructure; (4) prepositioned equipment; and (5) building partner capacity. The Department of Defense initiated the **Atlantic Resolve** mission to carry out these activities, many of which were focused on the Baltic States. All NATO allies joined the United States in contributing to reassurance efforts and, at the September 2014 NATO Summit in Wales, established the **Readiness Action Plan**—a series of 17 assurance and adaptation measures, including the **Very High Readiness Joint Task Force (VJTF)**, that aimed to make the alliance more resilient and responsive to threats. At the same summit, allies pledged to increase their defense investment in line with the alliance's two percent spending target. This was the first time allies agreed to move toward the spending target at the level of heads of state and government.

As the initial surprise of Ukraine faded, the United States began to move away from a crisis-driven surge mentality to a more considered approach focused on strengthening the U.S. military in Europe after decades of withdraw. While work on this front remains, former President Obama's FY 2017 request for $3.4 billion in ERI funding advances what will be a long-term rebuilding process. NATO, likewise, has continued to calibrate and strengthen its activities under the Readiness Action Plan. The July 2016 NATO Summit in Warsaw announced the formation of the **Enhanced Forward Presence (eFP)**, four multinational battalions that will act as a persistently present "tripwire" force in the Baltic States and Poland. NATO allies have also made noteworthy progress on increasing their defense spending, with NATO Secretary General Jens Stoltenberg announcing in February 2017 that non-U.S. NATO defense spending had increased by 3.8 percent in real terms in 2016, or approximately $10 billion.[8] This is only the beginning of what will need to be sustained progress toward better burden-sharing across the alliance.

There are two competing concepts of deterrence that are key to understanding why the United States and NATO took the steps described above, and why there exists such a variety of opinions regarding the appropriate size and composition of U.S. and allied forces in the Baltic States. The first is deterrence-by-punishment; the second is deterrence-by-denial.

- A **deterrence-by-punishment** strategy requires threatening severe and plausible consequences for aggression, such that Russia sees more disadvantages than it sees advantages. A successful approach may mean that Russia perceives that it could attack the Baltic States and at least initially succeed in overrunning and occupying them. However, Russia would also be aware that the U.S. and NATO response would be so fierce and costly that the benefits would not be worth the cost. Such a strategy necessitates the commitment of

---

[8] Jens Stoltenberg, "Pre-ministerial press conference," (press conference, Brussels, Belgium, February 15, 2017), http://www.nato.int/cps/en/natohq/opinions_141005.htm.

a relatively small number of allied forces in the Baltic States, with the punishing effects delivered by allied air, ground, and naval forces arriving from elsewhere, as well as in the form of substantial resistance from local forces. Economic and political tools would also likely be drawn upon to isolate and further punish Russia.

- By contrast, **deterrence-by-denial** entails a strategy based upon blocking an adversary from achieving its goals in the first place; i.e., deterring Russia from attacking the Baltic States by making them confident that they would lose any such a fight. To attain deterrence of this sort, U.S. and allied forces should be persistently deployed to the Baltics in numbers large enough to make Russia believe that it would face certain defeat should it attempt any aggression.

I do not consider deterrence-by-denial either advisable from a strategic perspective or feasible from a force structure and resourcing perspective, especially considering (1) the extraordinarily high number of forces, costs, and tradeoffs that would be required to make such an approach credible against the large Russian military; and (2) the inability of the small Baltic States to absorb and support the number of forces that would be required. Deterrence-by-punishment is adequate, even more so due to the low probability of an attack on the Baltic States and Moscow's well-placed fear of NATO capabilities.

The United States and NATO have prudently embarked on a deterrence-by-punishment strategy to ward off conventional Russian aggression against Eastern Europe. This strategy is based upon a *reinforcement* model that depends on small, yet capable, **tripwire forces, rapid-response forces** that can be mobilized on short notice, and the ability to get **follow-on forces** to the fight quickly.[9] While much of the alliance's focus has been on ground forces, the United States and its allies would also be expected to surge air and naval forces to the region in a crisis, both of which add significant capabilities to counter Russia.

- As mentioned, the tripwire forces in the Baltic States and Poland are known as NATO's **Enhanced Forward Presence**, which began deploying in February 2017. The eFP is comprised of four multinational battalions led by the United States (in Poland), the UK (in Estonia), Canada (in Latvia), and Germany (in Lithuania), with contributions from several other nations augmenting or in some cases rounding out the deployments by these framework nations. These forces are complemented by the company-sized presence that the United States has provided to the Baltic States since 2014, but which will now only be present intermittently for exercises. Additionally, NATO has established eight **NATO Force Integration Unit (NFIUs)** in countries along NATO's Eastern Flank—the three Baltic States, Poland, Romania, Bulgaria, Slovakia, and Hungary—that will be able to act as rapidly expandable reception and staging centers for arriving reinforcements.

- The rapid response forces are comprised of NATO's **Very High Readiness Joint Task Force (VJTF)**, an approximately brigade-sized multinational force led on a rotational basis by participating allies; headquarter elements comprising NATO's Rapid Deployable Corps; and other immediately available support elements found within the NATO Force Structure.

---

[9] Lisa Sawyer Samp, Kathleen Hicks, Olga Oliker, Jeffrey Rathke, Jeffrey Mankoff, Anthony Bell, and Heather Conley, *Recalibrating U.S. Strategy toward Russia: A New Time for Choosing* (Washington, DC: Center for Strategic and International Studies, forthcoming).

The U.S. forces permanently stationed in Europe—the 2nd Calvary Regiment (Stryker brigade) based in Vilseck, Germany, and the 173rd Airborne brigade based in Vicenza, Italy—would also be able to quickly respond in a crisis, along with the United States' rotational armored brigade, made possible by ERI. Given NATO's requirement for political consensus before deploying the VJTF, the U.S. forces would likely be the most readily available first responders.

- The follow-on forces would be comprised of forces based in the United States that could relatively quickly fall in on the war-fighting equipment that has been prepositioned in Western Europe (Germany, the Netherlands, and Belgium). These **Army Prepositioned Stocks** were added under the FY 2017 ERI. Follow-on forces could also potentially include the full **NATO Response Force**, including its Initial Follow-on Forces Group and its air, maritime, and SOF components, along with any allied national forces joining the fight.

In addition to putting in place the means to support a conventional reinforcement strategy, the United States and NATO have also worked to support the Baltic States' efforts to increase their internal resilience against both conventional and unconventional threats. Such efforts, including Special Operations Forces training and arms sales, seek to make the Baltic States as unappetizing as possible to Russia by raising the costs of potential aggression and building their capacity to resist and respond to activities that may occur below the threshold of conventional conflict; e.g., "little green men" scenarios. While efforts could be better coordinated across the three states— especially as it relates to joint defense planning and procurement—each state has individually undertaken internal measures designed to better integrate their intelligence, military, and internal defense establishments. In particular, each state has renewed focus on improving the readiness and capacity of its reserve and national guard forces.

Challenges

A credible deterrent requires both the will and ability to follow through on threats and promises. In the case of the Baltic States, two commonly referenced challenges that could impede allied forces from quickly projecting force are Russia's extensive anti-access/area denial (A2/AD) network and, to a lesser extent, freedom of movement issues.

- **Anti-access/area denial** refers to Russia's "thicket of overlapping and redundant [defense] systems—including land-, air-, and sea-based radar, counter-air, and strike capability— stretching from the Kola Peninsula in the Russian Arctic to Latakia, Syria, in the eastern Mediterranean."[10] Allies have not yet invested in the tactical strike and other air and missile defense capabilities necessary to mitigate the risks stemming from Russia's conventional short-range ballistic and cruise missiles, as well as its advanced surface-to-air missiles. The Baltic States aspire to work closely with Poland—which is in negotiations to procure PATRIOT systems—to strengthen the region's short- and medium-range air and missile defense architecture, though concrete progress remains largely elusive.[11]

---

[10] Hicks et al., *Evaluating Future U.S. Army Force Posture in Europe: Phase II Report*, 34.
[11] Lithuania has, however, signed a $109 million deal in October 2016 to purchase two Norwegian Advanced Surface-to-Air Missile Systems (NASAMS) from Norway, with delivery expected in 2020. See Nicholas de

- Reducing barriers to **freedom of movement**—i.e., the ability to quickly mobilize, assemble, and deploy troops from across Europe to a crisis area—has been a key focus area for U.S. Army Europe since 2014. The challenges in this area are both political and logistical. Different countries have different diplomatic notification and approval standards for military transit and overflight, as well as different infrastructure standards, that make moving U.S. forces across the span of NATO's eastern flank extremely complicated. Allied agreement on a notification-only model, or a so-called NATO "Schengen Zone," for the transit of allied forces would be one way to minimize the bureaucratic burden encountered by U.S. forces and reduce response time. Other efforts include addressing logistical complications such as the capacity of road and rail networks to transport heavy military equipment.

A comprehensive accounting of all the security-related capability challenges related to the Baltic States is likely beyond the scope of this hearing. That said, I wish to briefly list a few other areas that reflect important deficiencies: the lack of sufficient operational-level secure communications and classified NATO computer networks; the lack of delegated authorities and clear rules of engagement for all four NATO eFP battalions; the lack of U.S. Status of Forces Agreements (SOFAs) with each Baltic State; and the lack of a cohesive regional assistance strategy that would help rationalize and prioritize U.S. security support.[12] Addressing these issues would improve the effectiveness and safety of U.S. and NATO troops in the region.

Conclusion

Article 5 is the bedrock of U.S. policy in the Baltic States. For that reason, it is difficult to disentangle our approach to the Baltics from broader questions of U.S. policy toward Europe, NATO, and Russia. Whether the United States and its NATO allies continue to honor their commitments to the most vulnerable among them will have implications for the credibility of the alliance as a whole. The steps taken since 2014 to reassure and defend the Baltic States have demonstrated unity and resolve to friends and foes alike. Statements or actions that equivocate or hedge U.S. commitments to the Baltic States and NATO will likewise resonate well beyond Europe itself. The new administration, with the help of Congress, would therefore be wise to continue to strengthen and build upon what has been done to date in the Baltic States.

Larrinagam "Lithuania and Norway agree NASAMS deal," *IHS Jane's 360*, October 25, 2016, http://www.janes.com/article/64881/lithuania-and-norway-agree-nasams-deal.

[12] SOFAs provide essential legal protections for U.S. troops, establishing their rights and privileges (including immunities) while deployed inside a foreign nation. U.S. troops operating in the Baltic States currently fall under the generic NATO SOFA, which is no longer sufficient given that upwards of 5,000 troops are passing through the region per year. See Hicks et al., *Evaluating Future U.S. Army Force Posture in Europe: Phase II Report*, 27.

Mr. ROHRABACHER. Thank you very much.
And, Mr. Rojansky.

STATEMENT OF MR. MATTHEW ROJANSKY, DIRECTOR, KENNAN INSTITUTE, WOODROW WILSON CENTER

Mr. ROJANSKY. Yes. Thank you very much, Mr. Chairman——
Mr. ROHRABACHER. But you need to turn your mike on.
Mr. ROJANSKY. Right. Thank you very much, Mr. Chairman, Mr. Meeks. I am enormously grateful to have this opportunity. And I have got to do this, the disclaimer: Personal views only, not those of the Wilson Center, which, of course, is a congressionally char- tered memorial to President Wilson. So we are very grateful that we can fulfill our public interest mission and participate in here. You know, I think—I understood your question, Mr. Chairman, about Russia's specific acts rather than just sort of vague general ideas of a threat and the reasonableness of American response as soliciting an analysis of how the Russians are thinking and why.
What do they intend, and is there evidence for their intent?

And so I would like to tackle that problem as directly as I can, and I break it down into three parts. Any time that I think about a threat, I try to break it down into motive, capability, and oppor- tunity. So those are the three parts I want to tackle in that order. In terms of motive, let's look at what Russia's actions have been against other states to try to discern a motive, vis-a-vis, in par- ticular, its neighborhood or what Russians call the near abroad. Generally speaking, Russians do not view other countries in the near abroad as fully sovereign. Certainly, not in the way they see themselves or the United States. Obviously, we know that Presi- dent Medvedev talked about a sphere of privileged influence; the Russians have supported separatists in Moldova, in Georgia; they have invaded Ukraine. This is well known.

In terms of specific actions against the Baltic States, famously in 2007, around the Bronze Soldier conflict, they intervened with cyber attacks against Estonia. In 2014, they abducted Eston Kohver, an Estonian security agent from the border, essentially kidnapped him. In Latvia, they have mobilized ethnic Russian vot- ers, stirred up antigovernment sentiment in Latgallia. In Lith- uania, they have mounted an information war disparaging living standards for Lithuanians and encouraging them to move to Kaliningrad, a neighboring exclave of Russia. And, of course, there's been sophisticated social media campaigns backing all of these things up.

Now, what do Russians want in the Baltic States? Basic motiva- tion. Certainly, they fear the American presence there, what it may lead to, but they like to maintain, basically, stable political and economic ties. Now, much is made of the Russian-speaking popu- lation. It is a tricky issue. Who is an ethnic Russian? Who is a Rus- sian speaker? In terms of percentages, we may be dealing with somewhere between 30 and 36 percent in Latvia, 25 to 28 percent in Estonia, 5 to 8 percent in Lithuania, depending on how you de- fine those numbers. Sometimes they are concentrated, like in Narva and eastern Estonia; sometimes they are very well inte- grated, like in the city of Riga, the capital of Latvia.

Now, Putin talks about the Russian world within which these people would certainly be included as being a major priority for Russian foreign policy and being the largest diaspora in Europe. He claims 25 million Russians left outside the borders of The Russian Federation.

And in 2014, in a speech in Riga, Russia's commissioner for human rights, Konstantin Dolgov, said: It has to be stated with sadness that a huge number of our compatriots abroad, whole segments of the Russian world, continue to face serious problems securing their rights and lawful interests. We will not tolerate the creeping offensive against the Russian language that we are seeing in the Baltics.

So does Russia intend to use force in the Baltics? Interestingly, most Russian sources say, no, they don't. Dmitri Trenin says Estonia, Latvia, Lithuania, and Poland are safe, even if they don't feel that way. The Kremlin has no interest in risking nuclear war by attacking a member state, and the sphere of Russian control to which Putin aspires certainly excludes these countries.

Now, Russians would have plenty of reasons to make these claims, but it may be that they have other motives and intentions in being threatening toward the Baltic States, like signaling to other post-Soviet countries. In particular, Belarus, Kazakhstan, part of the Eurasian core countries on Russia's borders. And most military deployments, if you look at Russian military deployments, are about exerting control and dominance over Ukraine.

Capability—I will keep this very short. Russia's military capability is stronger than it was, for sure. It comes nowhere close to what the United States can feel, much less the NATO alliance. And one of the challenges in assessing Russia's actual capability is the bread-and-toast problem, vis-a-vis, Russian troops that are simply always going to be in and around St. Petersburg and Kaliningrad versus troops that are there for the specific reason of sort of either masking or preparing for an attack on the Baltic States.

But there are other capabilities of concern, nonmilitary capabilities. And, again, this comes back to the issue of Russian speakers. Russian television has been called a couch potato's dream, an attractive, even mesmerizing mix of frothy morning shows, high-decibel discussion shows, tear jerker serials and song contests peppered with news bulletins and current events shows that tow the Kremlin line. So you get the idea that Russian broadcasting creates a very sophisticated media milieu within which people are persuaded by the Russian world view.

But be careful not to generalize here. At the end of the day, Russian speakers, ethnic Russians in the Baltic States, they are people. Many of them don't necessarily like Mr. Putin, many of them have no desire to abandon their EU citizenship, which they have, thanks to being citizens of the Baltic States, and many of them tune out from politics altogether.

The last point—and I will end quickly here—on opportunity there is both good news and bad news. The good news is that Mr. Goble is exactly right. The Russians do not seek to provoke a conflict with the nuclear armed alliance in NATO, and as long as the Baltic States are NATO members, that is going to be the case. The bad news is that a crisis is still absolutely possible. A crisis is possible. Either imagine a scenario within which this ethic Russian or Russian language issue is provoked, even completely made up and then blown out of proportion by Russian media, there is a firm response from local authorities, and that results in a crisis. And the other possible crisis here is a military crisis. This so-called heavy metal diplomacy, a Russian aircraft coming close to an American ship or another NATO flag vessel.

So definitely, in terms of motive, capability, and opportunity, we are looking at a real threat, a real set of concerns, but it is important to see it in context. Thank you.

[The prepared statement of Mr. Rojansky follows:]

Prepared Testimony for U.S. House Committee on Foreign Affairs
Subcommittee on Europe, Eurasia and Emerging Threats; March 22, 2017
Matthew Rojansky, Director, Kennan Institute, Wilson Center

**Prepared Testimony for U.S. House Committee on Foreign Affairs
Subcommittee on Europe, Eurasia and Emerging Threats**

Hearing on

"U.S. Policy Toward the Baltic States"

March 22, 2017

Matthew Rojansky
Director, Kennan Institute, Wilson Center
matthew.rojansky@wilsoncenter.org

Prepared Testimony for U.S. House Committee on Foreign Affairs
Subcommittee on Europe, Eurasia and Emerging Threats; March 22, 2017
Matthew Rojansky, Director, Kennan Institute, Wilson Center

Russia-NATO Tensions in the Baltic Region and Beyond

I want to thank you, Mr. Chairman and Mr. Meeks, for holding this hearing today to
devote time to a discussion of U.S. national security and foreign policy interests vis-a-vis
Russia and our NATO allies in the Baltic region. These are, without any doubt,
important topics, which although much in the news over the past several years, have not
received adequate consideration through exactly the kind of sober discourse and inclusive
debate that this setting makes possible. I am very grateful for the opportunity to
participate here.

Let me now add the disclaimer that my testimony here today is in my personal expert
capacity, and that nothing I say purports to represent official views of the Kennan
Institute, the Woodrow Wilson International Center for Scholars, or the United States
Government. I add that last point of disclaimer by way of once again thanking you and
your colleagues here on Capitol Hill, and underscoring that the Wilson Center is, in fact,
the Congressionally-chartered national memorial to our 28th President, a scholar of
international relations, and the only U.S. President to hold a Ph.D.. So although my
views are my own, my presence at a hearing like this and our other work in support of
you and your colleagues and staff, advances the Wilson Center's non-partisan mission of
"independent research and open dialogue to inform actionable ideas for the policy
community." Ok, end of disclaimer and commercial.

The Context

I've been a frequent visitor in the Baltic States and the wider region, including Russia,
Ukraine, and Belarus, and I follow closely the media and expert publications coming out
of the region, as well as relevant reports in the local and international press. In 2015,
during the run-up to NATO's Warsaw summit, I served as a visiting Research Scholar at
the NATO Defense College. Moreover, in my capacity as Director of the Kennan
Institute, I have had the privilege to host here in Washington many researchers working
specifically on topics related to the security and development of the Baltic States, and on
Russia-NATO relations in the region stretching from the Arctic to the Black Sea. I will
base my testimony here in part on my firsthand observation, as well as on the outstanding
research of these scholars and others.

The concerns of the Baltic States as they have been described by my colleagues, the
press, and the Baltic governments are real, not imagined, and they are based on historical
experience, as well as present security and political realities. I can confirm based on
discussions with Russian experts and my reading of Russian sources that, as seen from
Moscow, most of the states of the so-called "near abroad," from former Soviet Central
Asia to Ukraine, the Caucasus and even the Baltics, are seen as less than fully sovereign.
These states fall within an inner ring of close scrutiny and pressure from Moscow.

That said, there is a pronounced difference in Russian perceptions between the Baltic
States, which are EU and NATO members, and other former Soviet republics. The task

Prepared Testimony for U.S. House Committee on Foreign Affairs
Subcommittee on Europe, Eurasia and Emerging Threats; March 22, 2017
Matthew Rojansky, Director, Kennan Institute, Wilson Center

here is to assess how Russians view NATO's enhanced presence in the Baltic region, and what, if anything, recent Russian statements and behavior tell us about Moscow's possible intentions going forward. As we undertake that assessment, let us clearly recognize our limitations: we can neither predict the future, nor read Mr. Putin's mind.

Breaking down the problem

What we can do is study patterns, and try to extract lessons. One key pattern is that for a threat of harm to be realized, it generally must represent the confluence of three main factors: an actor's motive to do harm, an actor's capability to inflict harm, and the opportunity to do so—motive, capability, and opportunity. This is the basic three-part framework I will adopt in assessing the threat or potential threat of Russian action against the Baltic States.

In the context of complex internal diplomacy within the NATO alliance, and within bilateral relationships between the U.S. and its European allies, it is especially important to try to establish common reference points for analyzing the threats and challenges we face, and for assessing what may be the appropriate response. That can be difficult since where you sit—or in this case where you lie on the map—has a big effect on where you stand in terms of threat perceptions and priorities. But it does not serve U.S. interests for the transatlantic community to be divided along geographic or other lines, so examining and refining our common understanding of this complex issue is a decidedly worthwhile effort.

Russia's Motives

Let us first consider the question of motive—why might Moscow seek to interfere in the Baltic region, and why not? Certainly, the most acute fears of those in the Baltic States and beyond that Russia may seek to intervene were exacerbated by Russia's military actions against Georgia in 2008 and against Ukraine in 2014, both with continuing consequences for the sovereignty and stability of those countries. Russia continues to support separatists in Moldova's breakaway Transnistria region, and has shown an increasing willingness to meddle in the domestic politics of even well-established Western democracies, such as Germany and France. The allegations of Russian hacking and meddling in the 2016 U.S. election deepen this concern.

For security officials and political leaders in the Baltic States, none of this is new. Their view of Russia's hostile motives has been shaped by experience. Consider the 2007 cyber-attacks on Estonian state servers amid a dispute over the Bronze Soldier of Tallinn, and the kidnapping in September 2014 of Estonian security officer Eston Kohver by Russian agents; accusations by Latvian officials that Russia has mounted a vast and sophisticated disinformation campaign to sway the votes of some half a million Russian speakers in the country in recent and upcoming elections; and the statement by the head of Lithuania's Counter-Intelligence State Security Department, Darius Jauniskis that, "we are already at war, and for many years."[1]

Prepared Testimony for U.S. House Committee on Foreign Affairs
Subcommittee on Europe, Eurasia and Emerging Threats; March 22, 2017
Matthew Rojansky, Director, Kennan Institute, Wilson Center

It should be beyond doubt that Russians view the Baltic States as fair game for the kind of cyber and information operations that are becoming the new normal in what has been called "hybrid" conflict between Russia and the West. Yet, close examination of Russian sources gives little indication that Moscow seeks to escalate these measures to the level of aggressive military action, let alone the type of invasion or occupation that has been much discussed and much feared among NATO allies.

Russia has both broad and deep ties with the Baltic States, especially with the region's commercial hubs, such as Latvia's capital Riga, and with heavily ethnic Russian enclaves, such as Narva in Estonia. Russian experts describe their interests in the Baltic States as diverse and varied, but they identify three common elements. First, they acknowledge fears about U.S. foreign policy objectives in the region—fears which have been magnified by the increased U.S. and NATO attention to the region. Second, they seek to maintain a stable status quo in political and economic relations, including clearly demarcated borders, unimpeded access to the Russian exclave of Kaliningrad, and restoration of modest but important trade ties with each of the Baltic States, which have been constrained by E.U. sanctions following the Ukraine crisis and Russian counter-sanctions.

The third significant Russian interest in the Baltic States—asserting the right to protect Russian speakers abroad—is a source of acute concern. In 2008, then-Russian President Dmitry Medvedev claimed a sphere of "privileged" influence around Russia's borders, which many understood to include the Baltic region, while a major theme of Vladimir Putin's third presidential term, since 2012, has been championing the interests of the so-called "Russian World," including his assertion that some 25 million ethnic Russians were left outside Russia's borders when the Soviet Union collapsed in 1991. In the run-up to Russia's invasion of Ukraine, and afterward, Russian officials have talked of the need to protect Russian speakers outside Russia, including in the Baltic States.

During a meeting with Russian speakers in Riga in 2014, Russia's Foreign Ministry Commissioner for Human Rights, Democracy and the Rule of Law Konstantin Dolgov said: "It has to be stated with sadness that a huge number of our compatriots abroad, whole segments of the Russian world, continue to face serious problems in securing their rights and lawful interests....One of the obvious and, perhaps, key reasons for this state of affairs is the unrelenting growth of xenophobic and neo-Nazi sentiments in the world." He added: "We will not tolerate the creeping offensive against the Russian language that we are seeing in the Baltics."[2]

Still, official Russians generally eschew explicit threats of military intervention in the Baltic States to protect Russian speakers, and some Russian observers make an effort to distinguish the Baltic case from that of Crimea, where protection of Russian speakers was Moscow's main justification for use of force. Dmitry Trenin, a former Russian military officer and political analyst at the Carnegie Moscow Center, describes Russia's interest as "not a question of potential influence on the Baltic States," but "simply a question of

Prepared Testimony for U.S. House Committee on Foreign Affairs
Subcommittee on Europe, Eurasia and Emerging Threats; March 22, 2017
Matthew Rojansky, Director, Kennan Institute, Wilson Center

national prestige. Why are Russian people who live there not equal in rights with the [local language speaking] population? It harms the national pride of Russians."[3]

Seen strictly in terms of Russia's motives and interests, the Baltic States have plenty of cause for concern. But this concern need not translate to existential insecurity, since Russians do not appear to consider the Baltic States on the same list with Ukraine, Belarus, or other former Soviet territories that have not become NATO and EU members, and whose economies and politics have remained far more heavily dependent on ties with Russia.

According to Trenin, "Estonia, Latvia, Lithuania, and Poland are safe, even if they do not feel that way: The Kremlin has no interest in risking nuclear war by attacking a NATO member-state, and the sphere of Russian control to which Putin aspires certainly excludes these countries."[4] Noted Russian defense analyst Ruslan Pukhov agrees, arguing that, "Moscow de-facto demonstratively ignores all NATO hysteria around the Baltic region trying to show that it is not going to threaten Baltic and Scandinavian nations and Poland and does not seek any conflict there."[5]

Why, then, do Russians pursue such a seemingly hostile rhetorical and political line toward the Baltic States, and why have they expended resources on cyber-attacks and information operations? It is quite possible that Russia's non-kinetic interventions in the Baltic States, and the bombastic statements of some Russian officials and politicians, are about sending messages for a wider post-Soviet audience. For example, following Russia's annexation of Crimea, the Belarusian government has clearly sought to lessen its dependence on Russia and draw closer to the West, and Westerners and Russians alike have wondered whether Belarus could be the next former Soviet state to experience a Ukraine-type "Maidan,"[6] "Russian hybrid war" or "color revolution."[7]

In this sense, although Moscow may not intend to repeat a Ukraine-style invasion in the Baltic States, it may be seeking to clarify "red lines" to the West and to its post-Soviet neighbors. Both Moscow and Minsk dismiss the possibility of a pro-Western popular uprising in Belarus as unthinkable. Yet the Kremlin is clearly concerned to ensure the loyalty of its closest partners in the so-called Eurasian integration process, especially Belarus, Kazakhstan, Kyrgyzstan, and Armenia. Rattling the saber to keep the Baltic States nervous may deliver an indirect but still potent message to others.

Russia's Capabilities

Russia's military modernization has been much in the spotlight since Moscow's invasion of Ukraine in 2014 and the launch of Russia's ongoing operation in Syria in 2015. By almost any measure, Russia's military capabilities fall well short of those of the United States, much less those of the NATO Alliance as a whole. Yet as a recent widely publicized study by the RAND Corporation has illustrated, Russian forces would be sufficient in a scenario simulating a conventional invasion of the Baltic States to strike a decisive blow against NATO's forces in the region.[8]

Prepared Testimony for U.S. House Committee on Foreign Affairs
Subcommittee on Europe, Eurasia and Emerging Threats; March 22, 2017
Matthew Rojansky, Director, Kennan Institute, Wilson Center

Indeed, Russia's conventional military dominance in the Baltic region poses a serious dilemma. As the RAND study put it, "NATO cannot successfully defend the territory of its most exposed members."[9] This is the case even despite recent rotations of additional NATO forces to the region. As Frantz Klintsevich, First Deputy Chair of the Defense Committee in Russia's Federation Council put it, NATO "deployed four battalions in the Baltic States and Poland. Those battalions are useless themselves however they [establish] infrastructure that further can allow for the increase of NATO troops near our borders."[10] Yan Zelinsky, a member of the Russian State Duma Committee on Foreign Affairs agreed, stating, "There is no reason to respond to these actions [which cannot] pose any real threat to us."[11]

Thus it is not surprising that, according to Pukhov, in the last four years, "in Russian regions bordering on the Baltic States, no significant action was taken to enhance Russian Armed forces." In fact, in 2009-2010, Pukhov reports, Russian heavy weapons in the Kaliningrad region were dramatically decreased, with only one tank battalion now remaining.[12] This does not mean that Russia has not changed its force posture in the region in response to its worries about conflict with NATO. In particular, Russia has improved its air defense capabilities in Kaliningrad, replacing aging S-300 systems with the S-400 series, and deploying Iskander ballistic missiles to replace aging SS-21s.

But Russia's capabilities should be understood in context. Russia's deployments and exercises in recent years appear to be aimed squarely at dominating Ukraine, and deterring NATO, not threatening the Baltic States specifically. Moreover, some of the capabilities of greatest concern to the RAND war gamers—Russia's air and naval defenses restricting NATO's access to the Baltic Sea—are practically indistinguishable from Russia's defenses ringed around Saint Petersburg and Kaliningrad. The heavy concentration of Russian forces in regions that border on the Baltic States also reflects the concentration of Russia's population and industry in those very same regions. In other words, as military analyst Michael Kofman[13] has noted, these are capabilities Russia will maintain and seek to modernize in any case, not necessarily to cut a path for conquest of the Baltic States.[14]

Of course, Russia also possesses non-military capabilities of concern to the Baltic States, NATO and the United States, especially in the realm of media, information and influence on public opinion. Concerns here center on the significant proportions of Russian-speaking populations in each of the Baltic States that are accustomed to receiving news and information from Russian-language media generally funded and controlled by the Kremlin. Although a majority of citizens in all three Baltic States understand Russian, populations classified as "ethnic Russian" are highest in Latvia (around 36%) and Estonia (around 28%). In Lithuania, the percentage is comparatively low, at only 8%.[15]

Russian state media broadcasts an interpretation of news and events that is generally more favorable to Moscow's interests and Russia's official perspective than that heard in local language news media in any of the three Baltic States. Moreover, in a sophisticated

Prepared Testimony for U.S. House Committee on Foreign Affairs
Subcommittee on Europe, Eurasia and Emerging Threats; March 22, 2017
Matthew Rojansky, Director, Kennan Institute, Wilson Center

modern media environment, politically relevant news and analysis can be contained not
only in formal news broadcasts or articles, but in entertainment programming as well.
Russian television has been called "a couch potato's dream: an attractive, even
mesmerizing mix of frothy morning shows, high-decibel discussion shows, tearjerker
serials and song contests—peppered with news bulletins and current events shows that
toe the Kremlin line."[16] However, the extent to which such media exert definitive
"control" over public opinion, even among Russian-speakers, is far from clear.

In their research on Russian speakers in the Narva region of Estonia conducted in 2015,
former CNN Moscow Bureau Chief Jill Dougherty[17] and Estonian researcher Riina
Kaljurand pointed out that the divide between ethnic Russians and ethnic Estonians was
more keenly felt in the aftermath of the Ukraine conflict than before. Although the label
"Russian" is not precise in sociological polling, data reflects generally more critical
views of the Estonian government, of NATO, and of the United States on the part of the
Russian minority population. These views generally tracked with criticism of the
Estonian government's policies towards Russian-language schools and so-called
"stateless persons" (Russian-speakers in Estonia who have not passed the Estonian
language test required to receive full Estonian citizenship).[18]

Yet, as Dougherty and Kaljurand argue, the sociological data do not tell the whole story:
"behind every number and every percentage there is a person with his/her personal view,
perception and understanding."[19] Many Russian-speaking Estonians, they write, would
prefer not to choose between loyalty to their motherland (Russia) and their adopted home
(Estonia), they do not love Putin, and they tune out from politics in general. A similar
argument can be made in Latvia and Lithuania, where by definition, ethnic Russian
citizens choose to stay put and keep the benefits of citizenship and residence in relatively
prosperous EU member countries, even though they have the right under Russian law to
move to Russia and receive Russian citizenship.

In some cases, the vulnerability of Russian-speaking populations in the Baltic States to
Russian media's anti-Western tone is exacerbated by the local governments' ham-fisted
responses. In Latvia, for example, Riga Mayor Nils Ušakovs was fined several times by
the State Language Center for using Russian language in social media accounts belonging
to the Riga city government.[20] His cutting social media response, mocking the State
Language Center, went viral among Russian speakers in both Latvia and Estonia.
Closure of Russian-language schools in Latvia,[21] and shuttering of Russian-language
newspapers in Estonia have provoked similar mockery and angry protests.[22]

Crisis as Opportunity

The final element of the threat assessment is whether there is an opportunity for Russia to
act on any aggressive intentions it might have towards the Baltic States, via the
capabilities described above or by other means. On this point, there is both good news
and bad news.

Prepared Testimony for U.S. House Committee on Foreign Affairs
Subcommittee on Europe, Eurasia and Emerging Threats; March 22, 2017
Matthew Rojansky, Director, Kennan Institute, Wilson Center

The good news is that the Baltic States look quite different from, for example, the Crimea
or Donbas regions of Ukraine. For one thing, the mere fact of the Baltic States' NATO
and EU membership causes the Kremlin to think differently about the prospect of conflict
there than it would in other parts of the post-Soviet space. As Alexander Golts,[23] a well-
known Russian journalist and defense analyst, has explained, the very fact that military-
technical considerations tend to dominate Kremlin decision-making means that the
unappealing prospect of provoking a military conflict with NATO over the Baltic States
is likely to trump political opportunism that might otherwise tempt Russia to intervene.[24]

Moreover, despite the relatively high proportion of Russian speakers in Estonia and
Latvia, these populations are reasonably well integrated, especially in the capital cities of
Tallinn and Riga, and they enjoy considerably greater prosperity than comparable
populations in Crimea and Donbas did, even before 2014. In part, this is thanks to the
benefits of the Baltic States' EU membership, a non-negligible benefit for ethnic Russian
citizens of all three states. Regardless of their political views, Russians in the Baltic
States are also cognizant of the cataclysmic consequences of separatism and civil war for
the civilian population in Ukraine, and self-interest would therefore argue more for
peaceful protest in the context of settled democracy and the rule of law, rather than
support for a Moscow-backed armed insurgency.

Now the bad news. A crisis is still very possible in any one of the Baltic States. The
sensitive disputes over local language tests for full citizenship, and Russian language in
schools, the press, and even social media could escalate relatively quickly and easily in
case of a triggering event. Such an event, whether real or staged, could involve an
alleged hate crime against Russian speakers, closure of a private Russian language
organization or publication, or even allegations of election fraud. Imagine a scenario in
which public protests by Russian speakers are broken up by police in riot gear—the
visuals alone would be inflammatory, even if the police used extreme care to avoid
casualties. The Kremlin could easily raise the temperature by exaggerating the harshness
of the government's response, insinuating an external (i.e. American) hand, and even
making up facts and allegations.

The other major risk factor is the proximity of NATO and Russian military and security
forces to one another in the region. As Golts puts it, "the most dangerous scenario is [a]
possible accident with ships and jets which is very possible as the result of the over-
militarization of region."[25] A Russian jet's low pass over the USS Donald Cook in 2016
is just one example of how such an accident could occur.[26] In case of an accident-
triggered crisis, the logic of military readiness and mobilization might force both sides
into a cycle of escalation even if neither began with the intent to provoke a full-blown
conflict. The simple fact is that in the current atmosphere of heightened tension
following Russia's invasion of Ukraine, Russia and NATO lack effective diplomatic or
military channels for managing these risks.

For now, the greatest "known unknown" risk factor will be around planned military
exercises and maneuvers, especially Russia's "Zapad 2017" exercise, expected to take

Prepared Testimony for U.S. House Committee on Foreign Affairs
Subcommittee on Europe, Eurasia and Emerging Threats; March 22, 2017
Matthew Rojansky, Director, Kennan Institute, Wilson Center

place in September. In the past, such exercises have fielded vast numbers of Russian and Belarusian forces simulating strikes on NATO targets in the Baltic States and Poland, including simulated nuclear strikes.[27] NATO will surely conduct additional exercises of its own, along the lines of the Polish-hosted Anakonda 2016, which simulated large-scale conventional combat between NATO and Russian forces.[28] Even preparations for such exercises may be misinterpreted as mobilization for an attack, or the exercises themselves could be dismissed as cover for impending aggressive action.

What is to be done?

In some respects, threat perceptions dictate policy realities. Having raised concerns about the military defensibility of its member states in the Baltic region, it is obviously important for NATO to demonstrate clear resolve and concrete action to address those concerns. The European Reassurance Initiative (ERI) appears to take a significant step in that direction. However, such action can and should be undertaken within the bounds of what is feasible in terms of politics and military science, and with a view to which measures are likely to be most stabilizing.

While not all NATO deployments to the Baltic region will be seen by the Russians as destabilizing, any deployment will be hyped as such in the media. Depicting NATO activity in the Baltics as threatening to Russia's own security can be a valuable instrument for the Kremlin to mobilize domestic political support—especially in the run-up to the presidential election planned for 2018. It is therefore important to distinguish between media alarmism and the more sober perceptions of Russian military planners and political decision-makers, like those quoted above. In the end, the task for NATO and the United States is to provide the maximum possible positive signal with the minimum possible provocation.

A further positive step is the restoration of direct military-to-military dialogue both at the working level, such as the "hotline" for de-conflicting operations in Syria, and in the two high-level meetings held so far between U.S. Chairman of the Joint Chiefs of Staff General Joseph Dunford and his Russian counterpart General Valery Gerasimov. Such direct dialogue can at least minimize risks related to miscommunication, accidents, and unintended escalation. Dialogue of this type should be continued and expanded specifically on the Baltic region, with a focus on incident prevention and containing escalation.

The Russians themselves have repeatedly said that they seek broader dialogue on what they call the "rules of the road" for major powers.[29] In their view such rules should contemplate not only conventional military capabilities, but also cyber, nuclear, space and other forces. Russians prefer to negotiate legally binding bilateral treaties with the United States, which may be a bridge too far in the current circumstances, but their initiatives to hold such discussions should not be ignored, as they can serve as opportunities to strengthen mutual deterrence and strategic stability.

Prepared Testimony for U.S. House Committee on Foreign Affairs
Subcommittee on Europe, Eurasia and Emerging Threats; March 22, 2017
Matthew Rojansky, Director, Kennan Institute, Wilson Center

Russians have in the past called for negotiations aimed at establishing a new Euro-Atlantic security architecture, underscored by then-President Dmitry Medvedev's treaty proposal in 2008, and related Russian diplomatic efforts.[30] Yet they have objected to forums such as the NATO-Russia Council and the Organization for Security and Cooperation's (OSCE) Permanent Council for taking up this issue. Moscow claims that in these contexts, it is presented with the West's collective position and is denied the right to negotiate or adjust it, much less to veto Western-backed decisions as in the UN Security Council.

Dialogue with Russia on inclusive mechanisms for European security is necessary, but past experience has proven it will not be productive without a clear consensus favoring such engagement on both sides. On the Russian side, this must entail recommitting to respect the sovereignty and territorial integrity of other regional states, especially its former Soviet neighbors. For the United States and our NATO allies, this means finding a way to think about development of region-wide security institutions and arrangements that are understood as complimentary to NATO, and not as a threat to it. This is not dissimilar from the challenge facing European states that wish to see the European Union play a more significant security role without eroding NATO's effectiveness.

The existing infrastructure of the OSCE is under-utilized and under-developed but grows out of the founding principles of the post-Cold War European security order, enshrined in the 1975 Helsinki Final Act and the 1990 Charter of Paris.[31] It is therefore a natural place to begin a serious security dialogue between Russia and NATO. The OSCE Permanent Council must cease to be an echo chamber for mutual recrimination, and instead become a platform for substantive exchanges of ideas that would not be possible in a less inclusive forum. The so-called mechanisms and other institutions of the OSCE should likewise be viewed not as cudgels to punish states for breaking the rules, but as instruments for confidence-building, and restoring working trust in the principles of Helsinki and Paris.

Such an inclusive security dialogue under OSCE auspices would be the most productive context for addressing acute concerns around ethnic Russian minorities, language rights and national identity in the Baltic States. The dialogue should include the most sensitive issues of Russian media's denigration of the Baltic States' basic sovereignty even after 25 years of independence, and the right of Baltic governments to define their own national cultural and historical narratives—but to do so in a manner strictly consistent with OSCE principles, and inclusive of minorities.

The road to a renewed consensus around the big challenges of European security will be long and winding. Before reaching that destination, the United States can support smart efforts to reduce our own vulnerability and that of our NATO allies to hostile media and disinformation campaigns. The best defense is, of course, the truth. However, given the sheer amount of "white noise" in the modern media landscape, truth can be difficult even for sophisticated audiences to discern.

Prepared Testimony for U.S. House Committee on Foreign Affairs
Subcommittee on Europe, Eurasia and Emerging Threats; March 22, 2017
Matthew Rojansky, Director, Kennan Institute, Wilson Center

New U.S.-supported international and local Russian language media projects have begun
to gain wider exposure and have enjoyed some considerable success. These efforts are in
their infancy, and may take time to begin significantly impacting public discourse among
Russian speakers in the region. For such efforts to maintain credibility, they must
assiduously avoid the temptation to match propaganda with propaganda, which will
damage the West's brand and betray the values for which the United States and NATO
stand.

While NATO has been wise to pay close attention to information warfare as a
vulnerability, it should avoid exaggerating the threat or its own response. A recent
NATO-sponsored seminar on "utilizing humor as an effective tool in strategic
communication" seems to illustrate the latter problem. Organizers touted the effort as
helpful to "practitioners," who "will find the case studies useful in their daily affairs
owing to an extensive collection of facts, examples and practices."[32] It is hard to picture
NATO security officials competing effectively with Russian media—or any media, for
that matter—in the humor department.

Though it should not be exaggerated or over-simplified, the threat of hostile Russian
action against the United States' Baltic allies is real, and must be taken seriously. A
comprehensive U.S. and NATO response to that threat should begin with clear
recognition of all its elements—from Russian intentions and capabilities to acute risk
factors. Minimizing the risks of unintended conflict and escalation is an obvious next
step. Finally, both sides can benefit from a serious dialogue aimed at restoring the
consensus around the Helsinki/Paris principles for European security—including the
balance between state sovereignty and minority rights, and the strengthening of platforms
and mechanisms for transforming mutually assured destruction into mutual assured
security.

---

[1] Andrea Shalal, "Europe erects defenses to counter Russia's information war," *Reuters*, January
12, 2017, http://www.reuters.com/article/us-usa-cyber-russia-europe-idUSKBN14W2BY.
[2] "Russia Sees Need to Protect Russian Speakers in NATO Baltic States," *The Moscow Times*,
September 16, 2014, https://themoscowtimes.com/news/russia-sees-need-to-protect-russian-speakers-in-nato-baltic-states-39450.
[3] Dmitri Khromakov, "Dmitri Trenin: Ukraina - eto analog Pol'shi v sostave Rossiiskoi Imperii,"
The Baltic Course, December 17, 2013, http://www.baltic-course.com/rus/opinion/?doc=85263.
[4] Dmitri Trenin, "The Revival of the Russian Military," *Foreign Affairs*, May/June 2016 issue,
https://www.foreignaffairs.com/articles/russia-fsu/2016-04-18/revival-russian-military.
[5] Ruslan Pukhov, "Nasha Karta Afriki," *Vedomosti*, July 15, 2016,
http://www.vedomosti.ru/opinion/articles/2016/07/15/649326-nasha-karta-afriki.
[6] Paul Coyer, "Near Revolution' In Belarus: Lukashenka's Balancing Act And Putin's Fear Of
Another Maidan," *Forbes*, March, 13, 2017,
https://www.forbes.com/sites/paulcoyer/2017/03/13/near-revolution-in-belarus-lukashenkas-balancing-act-and-putins-fear-of-another-maidan/#5ac8fc3277a2.
[7] Paul Goble, "Minsk Fears Moscow May Organize Hybrid War and Color Revolution in
Belarus," *Eurasia Daily Monitor* 13 (2016): 116, https://jamestown.org/program/minsk-fears-moscow-may-organize-hybrid-war-and-color-revolution-in-belarus/.

Prepared Testimony for U.S. House Committee on Foreign Affairs
Subcommittee on Europe, Eurasia and Emerging Threats; March 22, 2017
Matthew Rojansky, Director, Kennan Institute, Wilson Center

---

[8] David A. Shlapak and Michael Johnson, "Reinforcing Deterrence on NATO's Eastern Flank," RAND Corporation, 2016, doi: 10.7249/RR1253, http://www.rand.org/pubs/research_reports/RR1253.html.

[9] David A. Shlapak and Michael Johnson, "Reinforcing Deterrence on NATO's Eastern Flank," RAND Corporation, 2016, doi: 10.7249/RR1253, http://www.rand.org/pubs/research_reports/RR1253.html.

[10] "Nado ot oborony pereiti k nastupleniyu," Lenta.ru, July 13, 2016, https://lenta.ru/articles/2016/07/13/drypowder/.

[11] "Nado ot oborony pereiti k nastupleniyu," Lenta.ru, July 13, 2016, https://lenta.ru/articles/2016/07/13/drypowder/.

[12] Ruslan Pukhov, "Nasha Karta Afriki," Vedomosti, July 15, 2016, http://www.vedomosti.ru/opinion/articles/2016/07/15/649326-nasha-karta-afriki.

[13] Kofman is a Research Scientist at CNA and a Global Policy Fellow with the Kennan Institute

[14] Michael Kofman, "Fixing NATO Deterrence in the East or: How I Learned to Stop Worrying and Love NATO's Crushing Defeat by Russia," War On the Rocks, May 12, 2016, https://warontherocks.com/2016/05/fixing-nato-deterrence-in-the-east-or-how-i-learned-to-stop-worrying-and-love-natos-crushing-defeat-by-russia/.

[15] "Minority languages in the Baltics: a delicate matter," Mercator, http://www.mercator-research.eu/minority-languages/language-factsheets/minority-languages-in-education-in-the-baltics/.

[16] Jill Dougherty and Riina Kaljurand, "Estonia's "Virtual Russian World": The Influence of Russian Media on Estonia's Russian Speakers," Rahvusvaheline Kaitseuuringute Keskus, October, 2015, https://www.icds.ee/fileadmin/media/icds.ee/failid/Jill_Dougherty__Riina_Kaljurand_-_Estonia_s__Virtual_Russian_World_.pdf.

[17] Dougherty is a former Kennan Institute Fellow and currently serves on the Kennan Institute Advisory Council.

[18] Jill Dougherty and Riina Kaljurand, "Estonia's "Virtual Russian World": The Influence of Russian Media on Estonia's Russian Speakers," Rahvusvaheline Kaitseuuringute Keskus, October, 2015, https://www.icds.ee/fileadmin/media/icds.ee/failid/Jill_Dougherty__Riina_Kaljurand_-_Estonia_s__Virtual_Russian_World_.pdf.

[19] Jill Dougherty and Riina Kaljurand, "Estonia's "Virtual Russian World": The Influence of Russian Media on Estonia's Russian Speakers," Rahvusvaheline Kaitseuuringute Keskus, October, 2015, https://www.icds.ee/fileadmin/media/icds.ee/failid/Jill_Dougherty__Riina_Kaljurand_-_Estonia_s__Virtual_Russian_World_.pdf.

[20] The Mayor subsequently challenged these fines in court and prevailed, though this did not necessarily decrease their political impact. "Riga mayor is fined for using Russian on social media," Meduza, July 27, 2016, https://meduza.io/en/news/2016/07/27/latvian-mayor-is-fined-for-using-russian-on-social-media.

[21] "Russkii, marsh! S novim provitelstvom v Latvii obostryatsya yazikovie problemy," Lenta.ru, February 16, 2016, https://lenta.ru/articles/2016/02/16/bezrusskogo/.

[22] "V Estonii zakrili poslednie russkoyazychnye gazety," Lenta.ru, September 29, 2016, https://lenta.ru/news/2016/09/29/ruspress/.

[23] Golts was a Fellow at the Kennan Institute from January to March, 2017.

[24] Alexander Golts, e-mail message to author, March 16, 2017.

[25] Alexander Golts, e-mail message to author, March 16, 2017.

Prepared Testimony for U.S. House Committee on Foreign Affairs
Subcommittee on Europe, Eurasia and Emerging Threats; March 22, 2017
Matthew Rojansky, Director, Kennan Institute, Wilson Center

---

[26] "Navy Ship Encounters Aggressive Russian Aircraft in Baltic Sea," U.S. Department of Defense, April 13, 2016, https://www.defense.gov/News/Article/Article/720536/navy-ship-encounters-aggressive-russian-aircraft-in-baltic-sea.
[27] Stephen Blank, "What Do the Zapad 2013 Exercises Reveal? (Part One)," *Eurasia Daily Monitor* 10 (2013): 177, https://jamestown.org/program/what-do-the-zapad-2013-exercises-reveal-part-one/.
[28] "Exercise Anakonda 16," U.S. Army Europe, http://www.eur.army.mil/anakonda/files/MediaKit_Anakonda16.pdf.
[29] Konstantin Kosachev, "Pravila umerli, da zdravstvuyut pravila?," *Izvestia*, March 15, 2017, http://izvestia.ru/news/670458.
[30] Richard Weitz, "The Rise and Fall of Medvedev's European Security Treaty," The German Marshall Fund of the United States, May 2012, http://www.gmfus.org/file/2657/download.
[31] "Charter of Paris for a New Europe," U.S. Department of State, November 21, 1990, https://www.state.gov/t/isn/4721.htm.
[32] "StratCom laughs: in search of an analytical network," NATO STRATCOM, March 17, 2017, http://stratcomcoe.org/stratcom-laughs-search-analytical-network.

Mr. ROHRABACHER. In context. That is good. We will be discussing that as we get into the questions and answers.

And, finally, Mr. Lucas, you may proceed.

STATEMENT OF MR. EDWARD LUCAS, SENIOR VICE PRESIDENT, CENTER FOR EUROPEAN POLICY ANALYSIS

Mr. LUCAS. Chairman Rohrabacher, Ranking Member Meeks, and distinguished members, it is an honor and privilege to come here and give testimony to this committee on this vitally important subject.

I have been dealing with this issue since the early 1980s. My message is very straightforward and is contained in my written testimony. I will now go on to answer some of the questions that have come up in the discussion already.

Russia is a revisionist power. It doesn't like the way the world is at the moment. It wants to change it. It has the means to do this if we don't keep ourselves united and strong. So far, it is doing really well, much better than many people would have suspected. If you had been thinking 10, 15 years ago that we would be discussing a threat from Russia of the kind we are discussing now, people would have thought that was crazy. It is going to get worse before it gets better.

You mentioned in your opening remarks, Mr. Chairman, that we created a hostile military alliance stretching to Russia's border and put troops there, and the Russians don't like that. I think it is worth reminding ourselves why they are there. Why did this change? Why has this happened? And, of course, during the 1990s, we didn't have NATO membership for the Baltic States, and we expanded it for a reason. We expanded it because these countries were scared, and there was enough going on that they were right to be scared. After 2004, many people said, that is it, job done. Russia will not touch a NATO member, and there is no reason to worry about it anymore. We had no plans, no contingency plans for defending the Baltic States. We had no troop deployments there. We had no exercises there.

That would have been a stable situation, but Russia provoked, undermined, and subverted the Baltic States, notably in the Bronze Soldier attack, but in many other things as well. And so after 2008, the war in Georgia, President Obama said we need contingency plans. We developed a plan, and then we increased them. There was a huge jolt which came with the 2009 Zapad exercises, which practiced the invasion and occupation of the Baltic States and finished off with a dummy nuclear attack on Warsaw. That was a real wake-up call to the West.

Russia tends to do the things that it rehearses, and everything we have done, in a much smaller scale, since then, I think has been a response to Russia raising the ante. Russia is testing our will in the Baltic States. And the best way of guaranteeing that we keep the peace that we have is by responding to that with calmness and firmness.

You asked for specific examples. Well, I think the military exercise and, particularly, terrifying snap exercises, which happen at no notice and involve large numbers of troops hurdling toward the border when we have no idea, really, what is going on. And perhaps the biggest example, I would also mention the role of money in Baltic politics. And if you read the reports of the Estonian and Lithuanian security agencies, which are available on the internet, they list in chilling detail the things that Russia is doing inside those countries.

I would also like to respond to the idea that it is a big ask from the Baltic States. They want a lot from America. Well, that is true. But you are not just defending them, you are defending the whole international order. And if you are worried about America's leadership in the world and you are worried about America's leadership in Asia and you are worried about whether your allies take you seriously, well, the Baltics is high noon. That is where it starts. If you can't defend the Baltic States, your treaty allies, then you have no credibility in other parts of the world. So you are defending the whole rules-based order, not just the Baltic States.

And, finally, I would just point out that the Baltic States are not just consumers of security; they are also providers. They were warning us about this 20 years ago when we weren't listening. They see things that we don't see. They can go to places that we don't go. They understand things that we don't understand. And we, in my country in Britain, your country in the United States, and other NATO allies, we are eagerly and greedily lapping up some of this expertise, some of these capabilities they have in cyber, in intelligence, and other things, which fill gaps, stuff that we neglected, capabilities that we got rid of in the past 20 or 30 years because we thought we would never need them again. So they contribute a lot to us.

What should we do? Well, first of all, we have got to understand that Russia is trying to change the rules and be clear that we want to defend that rules-based order. It is worth it. It brings peace, it brings prosperity, it brings freedom. It really matters.

We need to raise the cost to Mr. Putin of his attacks, and I strongly endorse the point about raising visa sanctions on the Russian elite. We have no quarrel with the people of Russia. They suffer from this regime just as much as anybody else does, if not more. But we should say to those top 1,000, 10,000 people in Russia, if you preach anti-Westernism, if you say that the West is decadent, the fount of all evil, imperialist, horrible, backward, and so on, well, you can't then expect to launder money in the West. You can't expect to send your kids here to be educated. You can't send your families here for medical treatment. You can't come here on holiday. We can do that. That is not a quarrel with the Russian people. That is targeting the sanctions on the elite.

And, finally, I think we just need to do a bit more on deterrence. What NATO has done in the Baltics is very small. It is 1/10th, 1/20th of what Russia has done. It is already a game-changer. But just having a few more American soldiers in the Baltics would make a very big difference, because Russia takes you really seriously.

And I will finish off by saying, we should look at the Baltic States like West Berlin. There are many things in West Berlin we didn't like during the Cold War. I know you, Chairman Rohrabacher, were a regular visitor there, and it was tremendously important symbolically for us. We didn't try and defend West Berlin militarily as West Berlin. We didn't put a Maginot line on West Berlin, anymore we should put a Maginot line down the Baltics. We said, this is where it stops. This is the furthest outpost of the West. And by defending West Berlin, we defend every member of the Western alliance, and we should look at the Baltic States in the same way.

Thank you, sir.

[The prepared statement of Mr. Lucas follows:]

Written testimony to the House of Representatives Foreign Affairs Committee, March 22nd 2017

By Edward Lucas

Senior Vice-President, Centre for European Policy Analysis and Senior Editor, *The Economist*

[Chairman Rohrabacher, Ranking Member Meeks, thank you for inviting me here today. It is an honor and a privilege to give testimony to this committee and I would like to thank you for this opportunity and the committee staff for their work. I will give a short oral version of my written testimony and then look forward to taking questions.]

I have been dealing with European security for more than thirty years, as an activist during the Cold War, and also as a journalist, author, analyst and consultant.[1]

I argue that:

- Russia is a revisionist power;

- It has the means to pursue its objectives;

- It is winning; and

- Greater dangers lie ahead.

In particular, I believe that the Baltic states are the keystones of the European security order. If they fall victim to Russian pressure, be it military, economic or political, then the rules-based system which the United States has established and defended in Europe for more than six decades is over. The consequences of this would be catastrophic, and not only on the other side of the Atlantic. America's greatness rests on its alliances: no country in the history of the world has had so many allies, and such deep ties with them. If the United States proves unable or unwilling defend its allies, the collapse in its credibility will be this country's greatest geopolitical setback since Pearl Harbor.

---

[1] I have worked as a foreign correspondent for among others the BBC, the *Independent*, the *Sunday Times* and the *Economist*, and written for American news outlets including the *Washington Post*, the *Wall Street Journal*, *Foreign Policy*, *Politico* and the *American Interest*. In 1989 I was the only journalist from the English-speaking world living in Communist-era Czechoslovakia and saw the regime there tumble in the Velvet Revolution. I was the last Western journalist to be expelled from the Soviet Union, having received in March 1990 the first visa given by the new, and then-unrecognised, Lithuanian authorities. In 1992 I founded and ran the first English-language weekly in the Baltic states. In 2010 I coordinated the defence for my employer, *The Economist*, in a high-stakes libel action brought against us by a Russian tycoon who denied that his fortune benefited from his association with Vladimir Putin. I know Russian, German, Polish, Czech and some other languages. As well as the 'New Cold War', I am the author of 'Deception' (a book on east-west espionage) of 'The Snowden Operation' (on the NSA defector) and of §'Cyberphobia' which deals with internet anonymity and privacy.

I recommend that the United States and its allies:

- **Give up any hope of a quick diplomatic fix or other deal with Russia.** This is going to be a persistent and dangerous conflict. It predates Putin and will outlast him;

- **Continue to strengthen and reassure the frontline states, in particular the Baltic states and Poland.** We have done a lot, but much more needs to happen, in particularly in increasing the credibility of our deterrent.

- **Expose and punish the Kremlin's activities in the West.** In particular we need to deal firmly with Russian intelligence operations, to counter disinformation, to intensify visa sanctions on the Russian elite, and to block passage of Russian dirty money through our financial system.

I am the author of several books relevant to today's session. The first of these, 'The New Cold War', was written in 2007, at a time when most Westerners were still reluctant to face up to the threat the Putin regime poses both to its own people, and to Russia's neighbours. Many accused me then of scaremongering. Fewer do that now.

The message of this book was not mine, and it was not new. It came as a result of my deep ties to the frontline states of Europe. In the 1990s, a time when Vladimir Putin was still an obscure official in St Petersburg, public figures such as Václav Havel of the Czech Republic, the former Estonia president Lennart Meri, and Vytautas Landsbergis, who masterminded Lithuania's independence, all warned the West that Russia was heading in the wrong direction.

They warned us of the decay of democratic life there, of election-rigging, of the resurgence of the old KGB, and of the growth of kleptocracy. They also warned us that Russia had not abandoned its arrogant, unrepentant imperialist attitudes towards the former captive nations of eastern Europe. They warned us about Russia's toxic cocktail of money, propaganda and force, and its use of espionage to find targets and exploit weaknesses. They warned us that though Russia was still economically weak back then, times would change, and trouble was on its way—not only for them, but for us.

We in the West did not just ignore those warnings. We patronized and belittled the brave men and women who delivered them. Now the warnings have been vindicated. The Baltic states, before and after their accession to NATO, have suffered repeated economic sanctions, military pressure and subversion. We in the "old" West have seen Russian mischief-making in the heart of our political systems.

Yet even now many policymakers and analysts in Western capitals still believe that containing and confronting Vladimir Putin's Russia is either unnecessary or dangerous. They take an essentially pacifist stance, that military solutions are never appropriate, and that dialog is under all circumstances better than confrontation. I explain in the course of this evidence why that is wrong. I hope that my voice may be heard where those from the frontline states, still, are not.

In truth, **Russia is a revisionist power**. Accommodating the Kremlin's interests is not about changing outcomes within an existing set of rules. It would mean accepting new rules dictated by Russia. This is hard for many Westerners to understand, because we believe implicitly that the European security order dating back to the Helsinki process in the mid-1970s is stable, because all sides regard it as fair.[2] This assumption is profoundly mistaken. The Kremlin regards the Western-dominated security order as unfair and over-ripe for change. It also believes that conflict and competition are central to international relations; talk of win-win outcomes is naïve at best and mendacious at worst. As far as Russia is concerned, war of some sort with the West is inevitable; the only question is who wins. In this outlook Russia, crucially, has the advantage of strategic coherence. Its decision-makers share a similar perception of the threat from the West. They have common priorities, appetites for risk and assessments of our vulnerabilities. None of that is true on our side.

The stakes are high. Russia does not believe that its neighbours should be fully sovereign, with the right to make independent decisions about their geopolitical future. In Russia, a former imperial power with a long history of invasion by (and of) its neighbours, such behaviour is seen as an affront.

The Kremlin does not want to reconquer these ex-colonies; that would be prohibitively costly. But it does want to constrain them. Russia particularly begrudges the former captive nations of the Soviet empire their freedom, their prosperity, and their sovereignty. Their success poses an existential challenge to the stagnant and autocratic model of government pioneered by the Putin regime. The Kremlin also believes that NATO encircles the Russian exclave of Kaliningrad, a geopolitical trophy carved out of the pre-war German territory of East Prussia. This is strategically intolerable: Russia must have the capability to break this perceived encirclement. Russia's security, therefore, depends on its neighbours' insecurity.

---

[2] The Helsinki Final Act of 1975 established that borders in Europe would never again be changed by force. The Paris Charter of 1990 established common principles of political freedom, human rights and the rule of law. The Soviet Union signed both. The Russian Federation is its the legal successor and is bound by the same undertakings, as well as the Budapest Memorandum of 1994, which guaranteed Ukraine's territorial integrity in exchange for its renunciation of its nuclear arsenal. Russia has flouted all these undertakings, and more besides.

To achieve that goal, Russia must change the European security order, replacing the rules-based multilateral system with a bilateral one in which strong countries do the deals that they can, and weak countries accept the outcomes that they must.

A precondition for this is undermining the Atlantic alliance. Russia depicts this as anachronistic, unwanted and destructive American meddling in Europe. In fact, the American nuclear guarantee to NATO counters one of the most powerful elements in the Kremlin's military arsenal: its "tactical"—ie sub-strategic—nuclear weapons. Without America nuclear, intelligence, cyber and conventional capabilities, Europe would be, at least in the short term, largely defenceless.

Russia for now is therefore concentrating on stoking anti-Americanism in Europe (such as paranoia about NSA intelligence-gathering) and anti-European sentiment in the United States. This could be termed "system warfare": the long-term delegitimization of the system on which Western military strength is based.

Russia controls the strategic initiative more than its relative economic and military strength would suggest. It is also in a hurry. The clock is ticking against it. Low oil prices mean that Russia cannot modernize its defence budget as it wishes. It faces continued declines in infrastructure, population, public services and competitiveness.

Russia could therefore decide accelerate this erosion of Western unity by provoking a crisis. A rapid, confusing and ambiguous series of events, quite possibly in the Baltic states, might prompt an insufficient, belated reaction from NATO and the U.S.—or none at all. Russia would then, in effect, have defeated its far stronger Western military adversaries, chiefly by dexterity and bluff.

The easiest way to beat an opponent is to break his will to resist by non-military means. That is Russia's favoured course of action. However, if the Kremlin perceives it has a decisive military advantage, it will exploit it ruthlessly, aiming to destroy its opponents' armed forces and war-fighting capability. This creates the danger of a "hot" war with Russia: something which Western strategic thinking has largely discounted in the past 25 years.

For this reason I particularly welcome this committee's focus on the Baltic states of Estonia, Latvia and Lithuania. As stable, prosperous, law-governed democracies, they are beacons of Western values. I do not need to remind this committee that these three countries are loyal American allies and NATO members. They are our frontline states: the future of the world we have taken for granted since 1991 hangs on their fate. If they are successfully attacked or humiliated, NATO, and the United States, lose their credibility overnight: a huge victory for Russia.

These countries are inherently vulnerable to military and non-military attack. Geography is against them: they comprise a thin, flat strip of land, lightly populated, with few natural frontiers and little strategic depth. Their economies are liable to Russian pressure. Estonia and Latvia are also potentially subject to Russian interference because of their ethnic make-up (between a quarter and a third of their populations self-identify as 'Russian' in some sense). Lithuania could face demands from Russia for a corridor across its territory to the Kaliningrad exclave.

Like West Berlin in cold war days, the military defence of the Baltic states is difficult, but not impossible. NATO has lately improved its plans and force posture in the region. But we should not fool ourselves: we have turned tripwires into speed bumps and road blocks. We have not committed sufficient forces in the region to deter a full-scale Russian attack. Nor, as I argue later, should we. Our deterrent should be much wider, deeper, more resilient and more intimidating than whatever we choose to deploy in the frontline states.

Russia has **the means to pursue its revisionist approach.** Russia has a "multi-model" approach to conflict with the West, involving the flexible and adaptive use of military and non-military capabilities.

It uses **money**, bolstering self-interested commercial and financial lobbies which profit from doing business with Russia and fears any cooling in political ties. Austrian banks, German industrial exporters, French defence contractors, and a slew of companies, banks and law firms in my own country, the United Kingdom, exemplify this. Energy, economic and financial ties constrain Western responses to Russian revisionism.

Russia practices **information warfare** (propaganda) with a level of sophistication and intensity not seen even during the Cold War. It uses the immediacy, anonymity and ubiquity of the internet to confuse and corrode Western decision-making and public life.

Russia is prepared to threaten and use **force**, ranging from assassination to intimidation and military saber-rattling. In some countries it works closely with organized crime networks. Where necessary—as in Georgia, Ukraine and Syria—it uses straightforward force of arms, backed up with huge military exercises to deter any outside interference.

This toxic combination of money, information and force is often called "hybrid war" Russia wages it both in the physical world and in cyber-space. Russia's well-financed, tightly focussed and increasingly capable intelligence agencies play a leading role in selecting targets and carrying out operations.

So far, Russia is winning. Even after the invasion of Ukraine, the response from the West has been weak, late and disunited. The United States is distracted by multiple urgent problems elsewhere and many Americans rightly question why their country should be borrowing money to pay for security in bigger, richer Europe.

That gives Russia, with its bold decision-making and high tolerance for risk and pain, great scope for future action. Foreign policy adventures—whether in Georgia, Ukraine or Syria—play well at home, where they distract attention from the Putin regime's failure to modernize the economy, infrastructure or public services.

Russia has a notable military advantage over us in the Baltic Sea region. It has A2AD (Anti-Access Area Denial) capabilities, based on sophisticated air-defence systems, which create formidable "domes" or "bubbles" over territory in which we need to operate. In effect, Russia could during a crisis declare a "no-fly" zone over the Baltic sea, forcing us to consider whether we want to put our planes and pilots at risk, to launch a full-scale attack on Russian bases in Kaliningrad and western Russia, or to acquiesce.

Russia itself does not know if, how or when it might start such a conflict; we cannot know this either. We can say confidently, however, that both the timing and the means of the Kremlin's next adventure will be unpleasant and unexpected. A central thread in Russia's approach is surprise. The new cold war is not like the old one. Past events—including recent ones—are little guide to the future.

I do not, however, believe that a military conflict over the Baltic states is imminent or even probable. It is far more likely that the Putin regime, at least initially, tests our will-power elsewhere, perhaps in the Western Balkans (where Russia recently tried and failed to mount a coup in Montenegro), or perhaps in an ex-Soviet country such as Azerbaijan, Belarus, Georgia, Kazakhstan or Moldova.

Any such move would be a serious problem, and I would suggest that this committee urgently schedules a further hearing to take expert evidence on how the West should counter such gambits. But the damage to us, and the gain to Russia, will be greatest if Estonia, Latvia and Lithuania are the targets. We must do a lot more to guard against that eventuality.

Recreating our strategic culture

The first task is to see clearly what has happened. This conflict is under way. We can contain it, but not end it, because continued confrontation with the West has become an domestic political imperative for the Russian regime. At best we can deter its escalation. But the European security crisis will not be fixed with a few deft diplomatic touches and clever compromises. Coping with a revisionist Russia requires a fundamental overhaul. Politicians, such as those on this committee, need to explain to voters and taxpayers that we have moved into a new, costly and uncomfortable era, but we will never go back to business as usual. Anything else paves the way for future defeats, and sends a message that the kleptocratic regime in the Kremlin understands all too well: crime pays.

We should not assume that we can manage this conflict with the tools we used during the old Cold War. Russia believes it faces an existential threat from the West, and that it has for now the upper hand in dealing with it. It will not agree to accept limits on the interior movements of its forces, for example, or in the reductions of the weapons that give it superiority. At best we may be able to pursue a limited arms-control agenda, build better military-to-military relations, improve transparency and lessen the danger of war breaking out by accident. That will be desirable, but it will not solve the conflict.

Nor should we assume that "dialog" is the answer. We should indeed talk to the Russian leadership—far more than we do so at the moment. But we should first make sure we have something clear and useful to say. We need to understand the Kremlin's strategic calculus and to make sure that they understand ours. We should make it clear that our aim is simple. We will boost our security and that of allies, to safeguard them from anything our opponents can do. We did not start or seek this conflict. But if the Kremlin treats us as an enemy, we help nobody by pretending otherwise.

We also need to rebut the phoney *Realpolitik* arguments, which advise us to make the best of a bad job. We should accept the loss of Crimea, so the argument goes, do a deal with Russia over the future of Ukraine, and get used to the new realities, of a Russian *droit de regard* in neighbouring countries.

Such an approach would be morally wrong and strategically stupid. Securing a Europe whole and free after 1991 has been a magnificent achievement in which the United States, including you, Mr Rohrabacher, played a notable part. True: we made mistakes. We tried too hard to pander to Russia in the Yeltsin era, ignoring the growth of corruption, authoritarianism and revanchism. We overlooked Russians' resentment as their country drifted from the European mainstream and our vulnerability to the steps they could take in response. We neglected Ukraine, Moldova, Belarus and the countries of the Caucasus. We were bewitched by the Putin regime's offer of cooperation against Islamist terrorism in 2001. We have been frequently dazzled by the spurious commercial prospects offered by Russia.

But having made these mistakes is no reason to compound them now, by retreating into a grubby defeatism. Legitimising Russia's land-grab in Ukraine would fly in the face of historical justice. Are we really proposing that nations which paid the greatest price for the mistakes of the 20th century, and which the past masters of the Kremlin occupied and despoiled, should be once again subject to outside interference and oppression?

Russia is an integrated part of the world economy and of international decision-making on everything from space to sub-sea minerals. It cannot be simply isolated and ignored. But that does not mean that we cannot raise the cost of doing business for the Putin regime, both for its behaviour so far—and with sharpened intensity if it menaces our allies.

As an immediate measure, in response to the continuing aggression against Ukraine and provocations elsewhere, we should greatly extend the use of sanctions against individuals. The furious Russian reaction to the American imposition of even a handful of visa bans and asset freezes on those responsible for the death of the whistle-blowing auditor Sergei Magnitsky shows the effectiveness of this approach. Estonia has commendably and bravely taken similar steps. My own country is belatedly introducing Magnitsky sanctions at the behest of Bill Browder, the American-born financier and activist who employed Mr Magnitsky and has championed his cause.

The scope of such sanctions should be widened to include hundreds or even thousands of Russian decision-makers and policy-makers. It could include all members of the legislature (Duma and Federation Council), all members of the General Staff, military intelligence (GRU) domestic security (FSB), foreign intelligence (SVR), the interior ministry (MVD) and other 'power agencies', the presidential administration, and presidential property administration (and companies which represent it abroad), companies run by personalities linked to the Putin regime, and any banks or other commercial institutions involved in doing business in occupied Crimea. Such visa bans and asset freezes could also be extended, where appropriate, to the spouses, parents, children and siblings of those involved.

This would send a direct and powerful message to the Russian elite that their own personal business in the West—where they and their families shop, study, save and socialize—will not continue as usual. The more countries that adopt sanctions, and the longer the list of those affected, the more pressure we are putting on the Putin regime to back off.

The United States should also urge allies to apply much tougher money-laundering laws to keep corrupt Russian officials out of the Western financial system and capital markets. We can tighten rules on trust and company formation agents to make it harder for corrupt Russian entities to exploit and abuse our system. It is often said that offshore financial centers are beloved by the Russian elite. But the shameful truth is that it is onshore centers in Britain and the United States that make life easiest for them.

We also need to improve the West's resilience and solidarity in the face of Russian pressure. We need to press home the dramatic changes which the European Union has enforced in the market for natural gas, and discourage Russia from using its close ties with Germany to build new market-distorting pipelines.

European, British and American regulators are rightly concerned about the way in which Russian companies operate in the world energy market. We should intensify investigations of Russian energy companies which have mysterious origins, shareholders or business models. There are grave suspicions of price-fixing, insider trading, money-laundering and other abusive and illegal behaviour. My own researches suggest that these suspicions are amply justified, though writing about them is hampered by the costs and risks imposed by English libel law. In the course of researching the defence in a libel case, I met several potential witnesses who were frightened for their physical safety if they cooperated with us. The more that the our criminal justice systems can do, through prosecution, witness protection and plea bargains, to deal with the Russian gangster state, the safer the world will be.

Next, we need to revive our information-warfare capability. We won the Cold War partly because Soviet media lied as a matter of course, and ours did not. They tried to close off their societies from the free flow of information. We did not. In the end, their tactics backfired. Just as we have underestimated the potential effect of Russian energy, money and military firepower, so too have we neglected the information front. Russian propaganda channels are well-financed and have made powerful inroads into our media space. They create a subtle and effective parallel narrative of world events, in which the we in the West are the villains, mainstream thinking is inherently untrustworthy, and Russia is a victim of injustice and aggression, not its perpetrator.

Combatting this will require a major effort of time, money and willpower, involving existing media outlets, government, non-profit organizations and campaigning groups. We need to play both defense and offense. We need to begin to rebut Russian myths, lies and slanders, highlighting the factual inconsistences and elisions of the Kremlin narrative, and its dependence on fringe commentators and conspiracy theorists. We should raise the cost of doing business for Russian propaganda outlets, by applying regulatory pressure—for example requiring them to register as lobbyists—discouraging advertisers from buying space on their websites, and by social and professional ostracism. Anyone thinking of starting a career in the media by taking a job with an outfit like Sputnik or RT should be aware that this will not be their first job in journalism, but their last.

We also need to start rebuilding the trust and attention we once enjoyed inside Russia. The collapse of respect and affection for the West inside Russia over the past 25 years has been a catastrophic strategic reverse, all but unnoticed in Western capitals. After the fall of communism, Russians believed we stood for freedom, justice, honesty and prosperity. Now they all too often believe the message they here from the Kremlin: that we are hypocritical, greedy, aggressive custodians of a failing economic system.

More broadly, we need to reboot the Atlantic Alliance. As memories fade of the Normandy beaches, of the Berlin airlift and the fall of the wall, and the sacrifice and loyalty of past generations, our reservoir of shared sentiment is running dry. Without economic, political and cultural commonality, the Kremlin's games of divide and rule will succeed. This will require renewed and extraordinary efforts on both sides of the Atlantic.

As I have argued, Russia is far too weak for a full-scale military conflict with the West. Instead it uses the more potent weapons, of the kind already seen in Ukraine: the confusing and fast-changing combination of regular and irregular forces, economic sanctions, energy blockades, political destabilization, attacks on computers and networks, and information warfare. In other words, the Kremlin chimera blends military, criminal, intelligence, business, diplomatic, media, cyber and political elements.

Traditional defence planning struggles to deal with this. We are scrambling to create the new, sophisticated and resilient means of defending ourselves that we need. We have plenty to learn from the frontline states here. All three Baltic countries have intelligence and analytical insights into Russia which big Western services struggle to match. Estonia's work on cyber-resilience, Latvia's on analysing Russian propaganda, and Lithuania's on visualising information-warfare attacks are among the best anywhere in NATO. I am proud that CEPA this week is hosting colleagues from the NATO Strategic Communications Centre of Excellence in Riga; we will jointly be briefing the National Security Council, the State Department, Congressional staffers and other parts of the U.S. government.

Our military presence in the Baltic states has become better since Russia's attack on Ukraine, but the steps we have taken consist of necessary rather than sufficient conditions. The Enhanced Forward Presence deployments in Estonia (led by Britain), Latvia (Canada) and Lithuania (Germany) still lack air defences. Many other gaps need to be plugged.

Russia complains about what have done and are planning to do. This strengthens, not weakens, my argument. The fact that the Kremlin is unhappy when its neighbors gain even modest improvements in their security is telling. We should explain to the Russian authorities and to our own public that when NATO expanded in 2004, we did not even draw up contingency plans for the military defence of the new members, because we assumed that Russia was a friend, not a threat.

It is Russia's behavior which has changed that. Ever since 1991, Russia has systematically menaced the Baltic states with air-space violations, propaganda and economic warfare, and state-sponsored subversion. The Kremlin launched a crude cyber-attack on Estonia in 2007. It rehearsed the invasion and occupation of the Baltic states in 2009, in the Zapad-09 exercise (which concluded with a dummy nuclear strike on Warsaw). Zapad-13, four years later, displayed a much higher level of military capability, particularly in moving large numbers of troops and equipment over long distances in short time periods. Zapad-17, this year, is still more troubling.

A further vital military component of security in north-eastern Europe is the closest possible integration of non-NATO Sweden and Finland into the alliance's planning and capabilities. These countries are not members of the alliance, so they cannot formally be part of its command structure. But we should make every effort to maximize their involvement and intensify cooperation. We cannot defend the Baltic states or Poland without their help.

But we should not allow Russia to frame the problem for us. If we over-focus on the tactical military difficulties we face in the Baltic region, we risk neglecting the revolution in our strategic thinking needed to prepare our countries and our armed forces for the task ahead. Our job is not the military defence of the Baltic states on the spot. It is the defence of all NATO allies through **deterrence.**

The best analogy for this is West Berlin during the cold war. We did not build a Maginot line around the American, British and French sectors of Berlin. We did not stockpile vast amounts of weaponry there. Instead each country placed a brigade in its sector to show that an attack would not be a military push-over. These forces' mission was to keep fighting for long enough for us to implement the contingency plans drawn up by the LIVE OAK planning staff: a counter-attack from West Germany—with nuclear weapons if necessary.

This was secret, but the Soviet Union knew at least in outline what would happen if it attacked West Berlin. It could have overrun the city's Western sectors at any point from 1948 onwards. But it wisely decided not to do so. The question now facing the United

States is how best to make it clear to Russia that an attack on the Baltic states is similarly unwise.

This does not require us to match Russia militarily in the Baltic. Nor does it require us to match Russia at every rung on the "escalation ladder". Russia depends heavily on the early use of small "battlefield" (often described as "tactical") sub-strategic nuclear weapons. Western countries have other effective deterrents, including for example, the JASSM and Storm Shadow missiles—stealthy, stand-off weapons, with large conventional payloads, to which Russian A2AD has no answer. Having worked out our military, cyber and other deterrents, we also need to work on the messaging: how to make it clear to Russia that any mischief-making in the Baltics will be unbearably costly.

Such specifics aside, better deterrence also requires:

- Better information—so that Western military and political leaders are not caught by surprise, or confused by a "hybrid" attack;

- Speedier decision-making—so that Russia has no chance to quickly create "facts on the ground" before the West has a chance to respond

- A clear US commitment—although the NATO brand is strong, the U.S. one is better. **My single most important recommendation today would be that this country deploys additional American tripwire forces in the three Baltic states, in addition to the excellent work already under way in Poland.**

A final footnote: whereas Russia once regarded the collapse of the Soviet Union as a liberation from communism, the regime there now pushes the line, with increasing success, that it was a humiliating geopolitical defeat. That is not only factually false; it is also a tragedy for the Russian people. They overthrew the Soviet Union, under which they had suffered more than anyone else. But they have had the fruits of victory snatched away by the kleptocratic ex-KGB regime. The bread and circuses it offers are little consolation for the prize that Russians have lost: a country governed by law, freed from the shadows of empire and totalitarianism, and at peace with itself and its neighbors. Our endeavors to defend our allies may also bring that day a little nearer.

Mr. ROHRABACHER. Well, thank you very much.

And I see we are on our own.

Mr. MEEKS. Me and you, baby.

Mr. ROHRABACHER. And me and you, baby.

Let me start out by saying that I apologize that this is not a balanced panel. You all have basically the same message, and we should have had at least one person to present the other perspective, and we did not. And I am concerned about that.

Well, I am here. There is only so much as to what I can do on my own. Okay.

Let me first apologize about that, because I don't believe this is a balanced panel. I mean, I just have to say, you all are intellectuals. You all are good sources of information, but we need to juxtapose your arguments with someone else, and we didn't do it, and so we failed.

And maybe we will have another hearing where the points that you have made, you could have two or three here, and maybe someone on the other side who could refute some of the points that have been made.

So with that said, let me just go into some questions that will be provocative questions, anyway.

I did ask for a specific military aggression and acts. I didn't seem to get any, frankly. I hear about the amassing of 300,000 troops in Russian territory, in Russia, is an act of an aggression against their neighboring countries. But amassing NATO troops and tanks in their neighboring countries, on their border is not an aggression. Talk about a double standard. I would think that that is a major double standard.

I will have to say that when my friend, my fellow journalist, a former journalist as I am, that I believe that the idea of declaring the Baltics like to be similar to Berlin demonstrates a basic perceptional problem of why we are heading in the wrong direction. The Cold War is over. As long as we are thinking about Russia as it was during that time period, and others, and Berlin, West Berlin, as being threatened, as it was at that time, in a government that was controlled by the Communist Party, that was an ideological-based party that wanted to create Marxist, atheist dictatorships throughout the world, replace democracies with Marxist dictatorships. That is not the world we live in today, and it is not the Russia. Russia is different than what it was.

Now, how different? Let me just ask for some specific things in the Baltics. I know there was a cyber attack, which someone brought up; I would like to ask about that cyber attack in Estonia, if you know about this. I am sure you all should. There was a cyber attack when the Russians and the Estonians got into a personality match when the Estonians said, we are going to take down the statue that is dedicated to the Russian soldiers who gave their lives in liberating the Baltics from the Nazis. And at that point, there was a massive cyber attack, which really was very extensive, and it was a heavy duty attack by Russia on Estonia.

How long ago did that happen? When was it? What year was that? When was it?

Mr. LUCAS. 2007, sir.

Mr. ROHRABACHER. 2007. And since that time, have there been any attacks of that magnitude in the Baltics? Any other attacks since 2007?

Now, I will tell you, we have heard over and over and over again about the incredible cyber attacks, and that was 2007. I am not excusing the fact somebody is insulting. France insulted us a number of times, and we didn't get so angry at them that we punished them. There are all sorts of stories about that.

We are talking that their 300,000 troops are a threat, but our NATO 30,000 aren't. Is the panel aware that we are part of those NATO exercises and there has been a number of them now. Part of that has been B-52 flights headed from England and then turning around at the Russian border? Does anyone here not considered that a provocative act?

Ms. SAMP. I do not.

Mr. ROHRABACHER. You do not. Okay. So you think a nuclear weapons delivery system aimed at the heart of Russia and then turning around right on the border is not hostile and provocative?

Ms. SAMP. It might be if they weren't doing the same thing to us. They are flying bear and blackjack bombers off the coast of Alaska around the outer edges of Europe. So the flights are a wash——

Mr. ROHRABACHER. It is not the same. Let me just note. What you are saying is ridiculous. It is not the same as aiming a flight of bombers into the capital areas, meaning St. Petersburg in Moscow, versus flying along a coast. Everybody has a right to fly along someone's coast. Now, let me ask you this: Are there also ships as part of those exercises that we had or do we have any nuclear weapons capability of carrying ships that were part of that? Any of you know that? Well, yes, there were.

Tell me, if we actually are bringing nuclear weapons delivery systems to the Russian border, you don't believe that is provocative. Does anyone else here agree with that?

Yes, go right ahead.

Mr. LUCAS. Sir, can I respond to that? I think one has to look at this in over a period of, say, 10 years, say we start in 2004, when we have expanded NATO and we have built quite good relations with Russia through the NATO-Russia Founding Act and the NATO-Russia Council. Things have deteriorated since then. But in each case, the deterioration started with actions on the Russian side, and we followed by much smaller actions on ours.

Now, you mentioned nuclear weapons, and it is an extremely important point. Russia has a very large arsenal of so-called tactical nuclear weapons, and these are integrated into its military doctrine and integrated into its exercises. And they practice getting these nuclear artillery shells, depth charges, short-range weapons out of the bunkers onto delivery systems. And they do this again and again and again.

We in the West have almost given up on tactical nuclear arms. We have very few. Those that we have are kept a very long way away from the Baltic States, chiefly in bunkers in the Netherlands. Our exercises do not involve their use.

It is a specific part of Russian military doctrine to do what they call escalate to de-escalate, which means if they think they are losing a conventional war, they will go nuclear. They make no secret about that. And they talk about these nuclear weapons all the time in a way that the neighbors find terrifying, not just the NATO members. They say this to the Finns and to the Swedes.

You mentioned B-52 flights. I don't know if you are aware of what happened on Good Friday 2014, I think it was, when a Russian flight carried out a dummy attack on Stockholm and on another very important military target in Sweden at a time when the Swedish Air Force had taken the weekend off because it was Easter. They had to scramble Danish fighters from Lithuania to intercept these Russians.

In my country——

Mr. ROHRABACHER. So the Russian——

Mr. LUCAS. May I just finish?

Mr. ROHRABACHER [continuing]. In the incident you are describing, did they actually penetrate——

Mr. LUCAS. No. They turned around at the last minute. And we also had a similar event in—and if you penetrate someone——

Mr. ROHRABACHER. So they turned around at the last moment. You remember that, and you condemn that, but you don't condemn U.S. B-52 bombers and nuclear weapons carrying ships going right to the Russian border?

Mr. LUCAS. Understand that the Russians are trying to make us think that we have no nuclear deterrence. And they have said, and they say privately and publicly, they don't believe that NATO deterrence works. And so long as NATO is a nuclear alliance, we have to show that we are nuclear capable. Now, we have many gaps on the escalation——

Mr. ROHRABACHER. Sir, I just have to tell you that I believe it demonstrates a double standard that will give the Russians a message that we are judging our behavior differently than we are judging yours.

Mr. LUCAS. Can I respond to that, sir?

Mr. ROHRABACHER. Yes. Okay. I am sorry we don't have other witnesses here to make these points, and I am going to have to give it to him. But I will let you answer that, and then we have to go on——

Mr. LUCAS. I just want to respond to your point about West Berlin, sir.

Mr. ROHRABACHER. Yes.

Mr. LUCAS. You said the Cold War is over. It is true, the old Cold War is over. But as I said in my opening remarks, Russia is trying to change the rules. Russia doesn't like the way the world operates at the moment. It doesn't like American leadership. It doesn't like the Atlantic alliance. It doesn't like multilateral rules-based organizations by the EU, and that is a threat. It is not the same as the Soviet Union. It is much weaker. But the symbolic bastion of the West is the Baltic States, because they are militarily vulnerable.

Mr. ROHRABACHER. Okay.

Mr. LUCAS. And in that sense, I think it is very similar to West Berlin.

Mr. ROHRABACHER. Well, let me just note that Great Britain seems not to like the EU either. Do they? Great Britain decided they might not like that as well.

And, yeah, the institutions that were created during the Cold War are beginning to, not evaporate, but to readjust, and some of them will disappear, some of them will remain strong, but this isn't the Cold War.

Let me just remind you, you are looking at the ultimate cold warrior here. I mean, this is not some guy who, you know, did not believe we should confront the Soviet Union. And I was deeply involved with that for 20 years of my life, actually, 30 years of my life.

Well, anyway, we will have a second round of questions, even though it is just the two of us.

Mr. ROJANSKY. Mr. Chairman, would it be possible before you move on to just add something on the——

Mr. ROHRABACHER. With permission from my——

Mr. MEEKS. Yeah. I was going to give you—okay.

Mr. ROJANSKY. I appreciate that. I just feel badly, because I think I was invited to try to elucidate Russian thinking and the conclusion of much of my research into Russian analysis and the statements of Russian leaders and the disposition of Russian forces has been that while there are real causes for concern—and that is why I broke it into that three-part analysis of motive, capability, and opportunity—that, nonetheless, we are not facing an acute, immediate Russian military threat to the Baltic States. And there are two principal reasons for that on the military side, speaking about nuclear deterrence.

One is that nuclear deterrence works. And the Russian sources I looked at were very clear that that is a big part of the reason why they wouldn't, under any circumstances, so assume plenty of other motives, potentially, to intervene in the Baltic States. The fact that you are talking about intervening against members of a nuclear armed alliance makes that—I mean, the Russian sources are very clear, they have no desire to provoke that, and there are certainly plenty of others targets that would be more desirable.

The second issue, and I made this point very quickly before, and I do encourage you to take a look at my written remarks as well, is this issue of disposition of location, that even if kind of politically and psychologically the Baltic States may have a similar resonance to West Berlin today, they are in a different spot on the map. They are just a couple of 100 kilometers away from St. Petersburg. They are, in the case of Lithuania, actually bordering on Kaliningrad on a heavily militarized Russian exclave.

And so what that means is, there is a certain amount of Russian military activity we are just going to see. We are going to keep seeing it, and it is sort of normal that we would see it, because that is where Russia's population is and that is where their assets are. So I think that is why in terms of context, I think it is very important that we interpret Russia's actions and threats, not with charity, but in the context in which they are actually taking place and not in a sort of fear-laden fever dream kind of politicized context. That would be my only——

Mr. ROHRABACHER. And, Mr. Meeks. Thank you very much for that.

Mr. MEEKS. Thanks, Mr. Chairman. And let me say, Mr. Chairman, I am sure the committee would love to have maybe General

Flynn or Paul Manafort come to testify, because they will have the opposite—you know, they will—hear their point of view. They may be great witnesses.

Mr. ROHRABACHER. Okay. Go right ahead.

Mr. MEEKS. Well, let me jump into this, because—and maybe I will ask Ms. Stamp, because we started and we were talking about that, because over the past 2 decades, since the end of the Cold War, you know, we talk about what we are doing or what—NATO is there, but the Russians have also engaged in exercises and have often quadrupled, is that not correct, the size of the NATO forces in the region? In fact, a lot of the Russian exercises have—you know, you have seen over 100,000 troops. And NATO, our Baltic allies have been—you know, they have been talking and telling us this for years, that it is not just something happening on one side, but there is a threat that they see right across the border, 100,000 troops unannounced. You know, they do this unannounced.

So my first question is, actually, has the U.S. military presence in Europe increased or decreased since the end of the Cold War? Two, is the post-Wales response enough? And what happens or what do you see with reference to the comparison of the exercises that the Russians have been going on for the last few years?

Ms. SAMP. Sir, thank you for that question. I would describe the scale of Russian activities as an order of magnitude greater, that is ten times greater than anything that NATO and the U.S. is doing. The size of the U.S. presence in Europe since the end of the Cold War has decreased dramatically. At its height, it was about 350,000 troops. That would have been in the late 1980s. We are now at about 62,000 troops. With the rotational forces that we have put in since 2014, that number has risen by about 6,000 rotational, nonpermanent forces.

And is it enough? I would argue there is more to do. I think we should seriously consider having at least as many troops in Europe now as we did in 2012.

Mr. MEEKS. Does anybody disagree, agree? Mr. Goble?

Mr. GOBLE. I would—Congressman, I would like to come at this in a slightly different way that I think speaks to that. I think we are wrong to both operate on a model that the Cold War has been restored and that the Cold War is over. The one implies that we are going back to a status quo ante of 1991, and therefore, we need to respond as we did then. The other is to imply that when you don't have a Cold War, the only possible default setting is cooperation, peace, happiness, and niceness with people. History suggests otherwise. There are competitions between countries.

I have tried to say in my testimony, perhaps not very well, I tried—it is clear in my written remarks, I think this is—that we need to address what Russia is doing less in terms of a military threat than in terms of the other kinds of threats it poses: Using subversive measures, using massive amounts of money. I would be far happier to learn that we were investing in more cyber attacks—counter cyber attack centers, that we were investing in more transparency in banking systems, especially, I would say, in the three Baltic countries, in Latvia, where the banks have been used as a major money laundering enterprise for Russian oligarchs, than to talk immediately about more troops anywhere. That is what I believe.

Mr. MEEKS. Let me ask this question, because I think in your written testimony, you do talk about the fact that you think the lines of communication between the Kremlin and the Baltic States should increase or they should be there.

Mr. GOBLE. Absolutely.

Mr. MEEKS. Now, given the subversions that you are saying is taking place, and given that, you know, we are seeing it and feeling it, you know, from the hearings we just had right here in the United States——

Mr. GOBLE. Right.

Mr. MEEKS [continuing]. As to some things with reference to Russia trying to get involved in our politics and democracy, do you think that, you know, that the suppression that Mr. Putin obviously has at home against the media, et cetera, and then the subversion that he is trying to do in other countries, will that ever change under Mr. Putin's leadership?

Mr. GOBLE. Congressman, the good news is Vladimir Putin will not live forever. That is the really best news I can tell you from this region. Moreover, Mr. Putin has changed his own approach domestically and in foreign policy terms several times since he came to—he was installed in power at the end of 1999.

Encouraging conversations has at least three effects, all of which are positive: First, if the Baltic countries show themselves willing to have such conversations and the Russians refuse to do so, the onus of not talking is clearly demonstrated; second, the notion that people in the Baltic countries are interested in talking—in having conversations with their Russian counterparts can be an important conduit of information and influence into the Russian Federation; and third, and this week—you know, this is something when I was working on Baltic affairs at the State Department 25 years ago, while the President of Estonia at one point famously said he would rather have Canada for a neighbor and that he wished there was a very large ocean between himself and the Russian Federation, the reality is that Estonia, Latvia, and Lithuania are going to be Russia's neighbors for a very long time.

Now, one would like that relationship to be such that Estonians, Latvians, and Lithuanians will make the choices about what they will do rather than those choices being made in Moscow. And that is what this is about. But the best way to do that, in my mind, as I said in my written testimony, is for us to be promoting those kinds of transparency changes domestically that limit the ability of Moscow to engage in the subversive activities which it has been doing consistently since 1991.

Mr. MEEKS. Let me do this. We have a vote that is up, and I know my colleague may have a question. And I did want to ask Mr. Lucas one other question. I think that the chairman had made a statement, and it is important for me to know also.

The benefits, you know, can you tell us a little bit what the benefits have been for the Baltic States to continue to be in the EU membership? And has the EU supported their liberty and independence in face of the aggression of Russia? And is there any difference—you know, and I think you being—you know, Mr. Rohrabacher indicated because of your accent, of course, and England, is there any difference of what you see the difference now with Brexit and NATO and the EU, and your opinion on that?

Mr. LUCAS. Thank you for the question. I am strongly against Brexit and I think it was a bad mistake by my country, but the position of the Baltic States is very different. There is overwhelming support for the EU in all three countries, and the benefits have been colossal, chiefly in the integration into decisionmaking, because in this rules-based format, small countries get a voice. This is not the Europe of the 19th century where the big countries do the deals that they can and the small countries accept the outcomes that they must.

We have people in the Baltic States in really senior positions, and making a difference, in the EU's decisionmaking. Very large sums of money have flown into the Baltic States, and the infrastructure has been transformed by EU money. The people in the Baltic States have the right to live and work and travel all through the European Union as European EU citizens. This is extremely popular in the Baltic States. And I think one shouldn't read too into British thing wnhich is very specific and very, very different. I just wanted to relate to one other point. You were asking about why there are no examples of military aggression in the Baltic States. Well, that is because NATO works, Chairman Rohrabacher. And if there had been military aggression in the Baltic States since 2004, we would have responded in military terms and——

Mr. ROHRABACHER. Excuse me. Can you repeat that?

Mr. LUCAS. Sir, I was just saying you were asking why there were no examples of military aggression in the Baltic States. That is because NATO works. You know, Russia tries other stuff, and my fellow panelists referred to some of the examples, and I could give many more. But we have drawn a red line in the Baltics, and that is a good thing, and everybody is therefore better off as a result, not least the Russians.

Mr. ROHRABACHER. Thank you very much.

We didn't have a big enough panel here. We didn't have anybody on the panel here to offer the other arguments. I am just going to have a very short closing statement and then I am going to have to run off and vote. We have a vote on right now. I am sorry we couldn't let this go on for another ½ hour and have a better exchange.

Look, I fought in Afghanistan against Russian troops. All right? I was a speech writer for President Reagan for 7½ years. One of the things my friend quoted was something I had worked on with President Reagan.

Let me note, I just think there is a mind-set, and it is represented right here on the panel. I am sorry, I am going to be very frank with you, that we are dealing with the Soviet Union now, except maybe for the gentleman on the end, but this is not the threat that we faced. If the Russians were doing to us, what we are doing to them. Our manned bombers heading straight into Moscow and St. Petersburg. No, it is not justified. It is provocative and it is hostile.

And the fact is that our Baltic friends, they don't even feel threatened enough to spend money for their own defense. So what does that tell you? That tells you that we have got people here, as well as there, that have a motive, in that they hate the Russians. All right? Not all the Baltic people hate the Russians, but there is hatred there for a just reason.

While the Russians controlled the Baltics, they murdered millions of people. And Russians were in Eastern Europe, and they murdered millions of people. And, yes, that is because they were there when it was communism. It was communism that motivated that occupation. It was communism that motivated Russians to go in different places in the world to try to supplant democratic governments with atheist dictatorships. It was communism; it wasn't the Russian people. And I will just have to say that the current Russian Government is flawed dramatically, we all know that, but it is not the Communist government that existed before.

Just this thing, I guess there was no other major cyber attacks that basically were able to cripple a country, except for the one in Estonia. I asked that. So I guess, as far back as 2007, we are going to start using that as an example of hostility today. The people in the Baltics don't think they are under military threat, because they don't even spend their own allocation for their own defense.

And, finally, let me just say that when I look at Russia, I would hope that we do not judge other countries differently than we judge our own. And I will have to say that the United States has military forces all over the world today, and in some cases we are places that we shouldn't be. And sometimes it is greatly important for our national security, but the idea that when a Russian spy ship comes down our coast, that we all go crazy about it and start saying this is provocative, which is what I heard in the news, but it doesn't make any difference about us having our warships, some of which can carry nuclear warheads, right up next to the Russian coast.

These double standards, we got. All I am saying is let's build a more peaceful world by at least dealing with the people who control Russia today, and try to reach an understanding, what is in your interest and what is in our interest. And today, we are acting in a very belligerent way as if, no, no, you don't have the right to do things in your own interest and to have a military exercise in your own country. We are comparing us having nuclear weapons delivery systems and thousands of troops right on the Russian border, we are saying, well, no, that is not aggression, but 300,000 troops inside Russia itself, its own country, that is aggression? This is nonsense, and we have got to, if we are going to have peace in this world, be realistic and we have to say to ourselves, how do we do this?

And it is not giving up territory. Nobody is talking about giving up the Baltics. But let's not say over and over again, which I have heard, the Russian aggression in the Baltics. I have heard that expression, military aggression in the Baltics, dozens, if not 30 or 40 times used to justify a hostile foreign policy toward Russia. And I will tell you, nothing that I have heard today justifies that phrase being used: Russian military aggression in the Baltics.

So with that said, I want to thank our panel. I am sorry that I was able to do this tirade at the end. I really wanted it to be an exchange where you could refute me, and back and forth, because

that is what we are supposed to have here, but I have to go vote
and my friend has to go vote as well.

I want to thank you very much. And thank you for putting up
with me venting at the very last minute without your chance to retort. But if you would like to put in the record a retort, we will do
it. Okay? Thank you all very much.

[Whereupon, at 3:20 p.m., the subcommittee was adjourned.]

A P P E N D I X

Material Submitted for the Record

SUBCOMMITTEE HEARING NOTICE
COMMITTEE ON FOREIGN AFFAIRS
U.S. HOUSE OF REPRESENTATIVES
WASHINGTON, DC 20515-6128

Subcommittee on Europe, Eurasia, and Emerging Threats
Dana Rohrabacher (R-CA), Chairman

March 15, 2017

TO: MEMBERS OF THE COMMITTEE ON FOREIGN AFFAIRS

You are respectfully requested to attend an OPEN hearing of the Committee on Foreign Affairs, to be held by the Subcommittee on Europe, Eurasia, and Emerging Threats in Room 2172 of the Rayburn House Office Building (and available live on the Committee website at http://www.ForeignAffairs.house.gov):

DATE: Wednesday, March 22, 2017

TIME: 2:00 p.m.

SUBJECT: U.S. Policy Toward the Baltic States

WITNESSES: Mr. Paul A. Goble
                 Principal Professor
                 The Institute of World Politics

                 Ms. Lisa Sawyer Samp
                 Senior Fellow
                 International Security Program
                 Center for Strategic and International Studies

                 Mr. Matthew Rojansky
                 Director
                 Kennan Institute
                 Woodrow Wilson Center

                 Mr. Edward Lucas
                 Senior Vice President
                 Center for European Policy Analysis

By Direction of the Chairman

COMMITTEE ON FOREIGN AFFAIRS

MINUTES OF SUBCOMMITTEE ON _____ *Europe, Eurasia, and Emerging Threats* _____ HEARING

Day __*Wednesday*__ Date _____ *March 22* _____ Room ___ *2172 RHOB* ___

Starting Time ___ *2:08 p.m.* ___ Ending Time ___ *3:20 p.m.* ___

Recesses | *0* | (___ to ___) (___ to ___) (___ to ___) (___ to ___) (___ to ___) (___ to ___)

Presiding Member(s)

Rep. Rohrabacher

Check all of the following that apply:

Open Session ☑   Electronically Recorded (taped) ☑
Executive (closed) Session ☐   Stenographic Record ☑
Televised ☐

TITLE OF HEARING:

U.S. Policy Toward the Baltic States

SUBCOMMITTEE MEMBERS PRESENT:

Rep. Meeks, Rep. Fitzpatrick, Rep. Sherman, Rep. Cicilline, Rep. Kelly

---

NON-SUBCOMMITTEE MEMBERS PRESENT: *(Mark with an * if they are not members of full committee.)*

N/A

HEARING WITNESSES: Same as meeting notice attached? Yes ☑ No ☐
(If "no", please list below and include title, agency, department, or organization.)

STATEMENTS FOR THE RECORD: *(List any statements submitted for the record.)*

Attached

TIME SCHEDULED TO RECONVENE _____
or
TIME ADJOURNED ___ *3:20 p.m.* ___

_____
Subcommittee Staff Associate

Statement for the Record
Rep. Robin L. Kelly
EE&ET Subcommittee Hearing: "U.S. Policy Toward the Baltics"
March 22, 2017

Thank you Mr. Chairman for holding this hearing on the U.S. policy toward the Baltic States.

Now, more than ever the United States must remain committed to the NATO alliance. Yesterday, I was disappointed to learn that Secretary Tillerson will be skipping the NATO Summit next month in Brussels. I hope this does not become a trend and that the United States will return to full participation at future NATO Summits.

The Baltic States lie on the front lines of likely future Russian aggression. Estonia, Latvia, and Lithuania have been prime success stories with democratic governments that were admitted to full membership as members of NATO and the European Union. These three countries have come to our aid in the past- contributing forces for missions in Afghanistan- and we cannot waiver to assist them in their time of need.

As someone of Ukrainian decent, I was shocked by the 2014 Russian annexation of Crimea and the incursion into Ukraine.

Currently the Russian military has around 400,000 troops stationed between Poland and Lithuania.

Following their success in Ukraine, Russia is likely to target ethnic Russian populations in the future and test NATO's resolve with an invasion in one of the Baltic States. Russian speakers make up thirty percent of Estonia's population. Thirty-four percent of Latvia's population speaks Russian as their first language. Russia understands this vulnerability and is already pumping propaganda and misinformation into these populations and seeks to generate distrust and division in local populations.

The Baltic States broadly welcomed the deterrence measures agreed to at NATO's Wales Summit in 2014 to form the Readiness Action Plan. Germany will lead the troops in Lithuania, while there will be a US-led deployment in Poland, British-led forces in Estonia and Canadian-led troops in Latvia.

In June 2015, Secretary Carter committed the United States to providing artillery, surveillance, and logistics and airlift support to the Very High Readiness Joint Fast Force.

Questions:

Mr. Lucas and Ms. Samp:

Have you seen any indication that this new Administration will not fulfill their NATO responsibilities agreed to relating to the Readiness Action Plan? If the US does withdraw resources, what would this mean for the future of NATO and how would this be interpreted by our allies around the world?

Mr. Lucas:

In the Baltic region there are currently hundreds of thousands of troops on both sides of the boarder. In your testimony you said that "Russia is winning" versus the West. Given their tolerance for high risk, high reward operations and past successes in Moldova, Georgia, and Ukraine, how can NATO best provide a deterrent force without being seen as a threat to Russian security? Given their propensity to escalate to deescalate, how do we avoid miscommunications on both sides?

MATERIAL SUBMITTED FOR THE RECORD BY THE HONORABLE DANA ROHRABACHER, A REPRESENTATIVE IN CONGRESS FROM THE STATE OF CALIFORNIA, AND CHAIRMAN, SUBCOMMITTEE ON EUROPE, EURASIA, AND EMERGING THREATS

MATERIAL SUBMITTED FOR THE RECORD BY MR. MATTHEW ROJANSKY, DIRECTOR, KENNAN INSTITUTE, WOODROW WILSON CENTER

Riga Mayor Nils Ušakovs vs the Latvian State Language Center

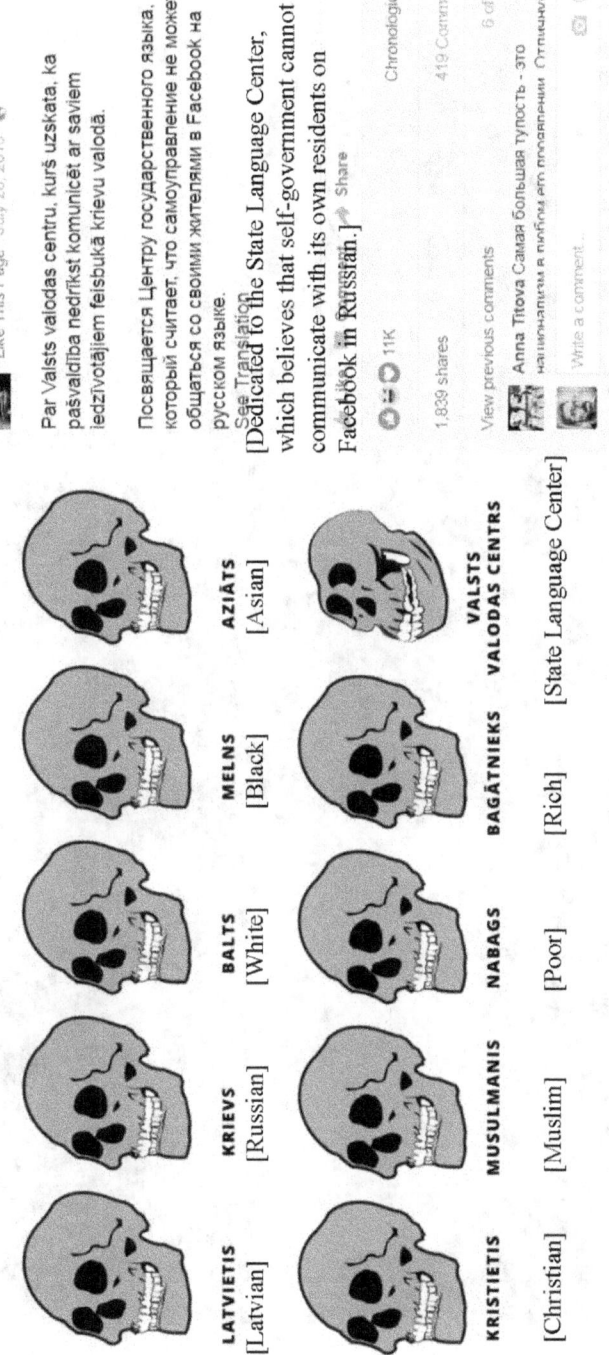

Nils Ušakovs • Нил Ушаков
Like This Page · July 28, 2016

Par Valsts valodas centru, kurš uzskata, ka pašvaldība nedrīkst komunicēt ar saviem iedzīvotājiem feisbukā krievu valodā.

Посвящается Центру государственного языка, который считает, что самоуправление не может общаться со своими жителями в Facebook на русском языке.

See Translation
[Dedicated to the State Language Center, which believes that self-government cannot communicate with its own residents on Facebook in Russian.] Share

11K
1,839 shares

Chronologic

419 Comme

6 d

View previous comments

Anna Titova Самая большая тупость - это национализм в публом это порождении Отпичии

Write a comment...

LATVIETIS [Latvian]   KRIEVS [Russian]   BALTS [White]   MELNS [Black]   AZIĀTS [Asian]

KRISTIETIS [Christian]   MUSULMANIS [Muslim]   NABAGS [Poor]   BAGĀTNIEKS [Rich]   VALSTS VALODAS CENTRS [State Language Center]

[English translation superimposed by Matthew Rojansky]

Note: A Russian language version of this same meme also circulated widely

Source: Facebook.com, accessed 3/17/17. Available at:

https://www.facebook.com/NilsUsakovs/photos/a.21332104203215 5.59458.212485185449074/1196301367067446/?type=3&theater

Humor Militaris....ad absurdum

Source: Cvent.com, accessed 3/17/17. Available at: https://www.cvent.com/c/express/349ed630-b15d-48ad-aa89-a4999c539c3a

Question for the Record Response
Edward Lucas to Rep. Robin Kelly

Question 1: Have you seen any indication that this new Administration will not fulfill their NATO responsibilities agreed to relating to the Readiness Action Plan? If the US does withdraw resources, what would this mean for the future of NATO and how would this be interpreted by our allies around the world?

Mr. Lucas: No indication of this so far—but there are plenty of worries. The Readiness Action Plan is the bare minimum for the defence of the frontline states. We still lack air-defence capability, and in the event of a conflict US forces would have to retreat to western Poland to await reinforcements, which would probably take 180 days. The best way of avoiding war is to make sure that our deterrent is 100% credible. The frontline states are reassured by the presence of James Mattis at the Pentagon, and by their meetings with VP Pence. But the damage done by the Trump campaign rhetoric remains.

Question 2: In the Baltic region there are currently hundreds of thousands of troops on both sides of the boarder. In your testimony you said that "Russia is winning" versus the West. Given their tolerance for high risk, high reward operations and past successes in Moldova, Georgia, and Ukraine, how can NATO best provide a deterrent force without being seen as a threat to Russian security? Given their propensity to escalate to deescalate, how do we avoid miscommunications on both sides?

Mr. Lucas: There is no equivalence between the limited and defensive NATO forces in the frontline states, and the much larger and more heavily-armed Russian forces We barely have the capability to defend ourselves in the Baltic theatre. They have abundant capability to attack. A particular worry, as you rightly point out, are the gaps on our side on the "escalation ladder". Russia has repeatedly said that it is prepared to use sub-strategic ("tactical") nuclear weapons in order to end a a conventional conflict. We in NATO do not have a full answer to this. Our stocks of these weapons are small and distant from the potential battlefield (chiefly held in the Netherlands).

I believe that the best answer to this lies in the use of air-launched stealthy stand-off weapons such as the JASSM and the European-made Storm Shadow, and the planned Long-Range Stand-Off (LRSO) weapon. These are capable of puncturing Russia's A2AD capabilities and their conventional warheads provide a substantial deterrent to Russian adventurism. I believe we should increase our stocks of these weapons (already held in the case of the JASSM by Finland and Poland), and develop more modern variants. We should articulate clearly to the Russians that these are part of our deterrent.

Question for the Record Response
Lisa Samp to Rep. Robin Kelly

Rep. Kelly:

Have you seen any indication that this new Administration will not fulfill their NATO responsibilities agreed to relating to the Readiness Action Plan? If the US does withdraw resources, what would this mean for the future of NATO and how would this be interpreted by our allies around the world?

Lisa Samp:

Beyond tough talk toward NATO in general, I have seen no specific indications that the Trump Administration intends to scale back or cease contributions to NATO's Readiness Action Plan or other associated activities. Much, however, depends on continued funding for the European Reassurance Initiative (ERI, also referred to as the European Deterrence Initiative), which affords U.S. activities in Europe and is currently covered by the continuing resolution. As of now, the Defense Department's efforts to moderately scale-up the troop presence in Europe, preposition additional equipment, and sustain or enhance other activities—as proposed in the FY 2017 ERI request for $3.4 billion—have continued uninterrupted from the Obama Administration to the Trump Administration.

There would be significant consequences should the United States decide to unilaterally withdraw from the assurance and deterrence activities in Europe absent major improvements in the security situation. NATO would view such a move as a significant concession to Russia, decreasing U.S. leverage in managing the challenge and inviting further aggression. The Baltic States, specifically, would view such a move as complete abandonment. It would send a strong signal to allies and adversaries alike that the United States does not intend to live up to its collective defense commitments and that there will be no punishment for acts of aggression. NATO, which relies on U.S. leadership, would be drastically weakened and Transatlantic unity shattered.

www.ingramcontent.com/pod-product-compliance
Lightning Source LLC
Chambersburg PA
CBHW081411280526
45788CB00009B/3064